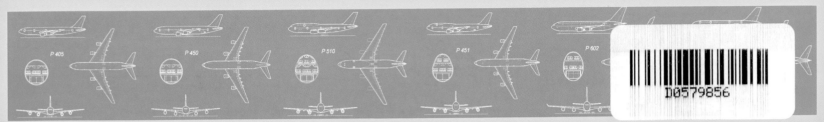

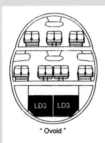
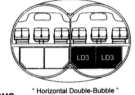
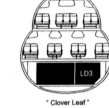

Possible Airbus UHCA fuselage cross sections

medium-haul business class configurations

" Ovoid "

" Horizontal Double-Bubble "

LD3 LD3

LD3 LD3

" Circular "

LD3 LD9

" Clover Leaf "

LD3

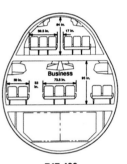
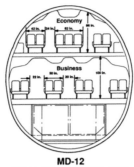

*W*ide-Body Cross Section Comparison

Economy

Business

Business

747-400
256 in. Wide by 309 in. High

MD-12
291 in. Wide by 335 in. High

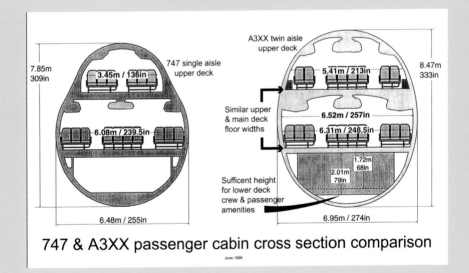

747 single aisle upper deck

A3XX twin aisle upper deck

7.85m 309in

3.45m / 136in

5.41m / 213in

8.47m 333in

Similar upper & main deck floor widths

6.52m / 257in

6.08m / 239.5in

6.31m / 248.5in

1.72m 68in

2.01m 79in

Sufficent height for lower deck crew & passenger amenities

6.48m / 255in

6.95m / 274in

747 & A3XX passenger cabin cross section comparison

June 1996

Status 3   Status 5   Status 6   Status 8   Status 10

AIRBUS A380

Superjumbo of the 21st Century

ZENITH
PRESS

Guy Norris and Mark Wagner

Dedication

To Mark Hewish (1948–2005), colleague, mentor, and above all, great friend.

First published in 2005 by Zenith Press, an imprint of MBI Publishing Company, Galtier Plaza, Suite 200, 380 Jackson Street, St. Paul, MN 55101-3885 USA

Zenith Press titles are also available at discounts in bulk quantity for industrial or sales-promotional use. For details write to Special Sales Manager at MBI Publishing Company, Galtier Plaza, Suite 200, 380 Jackson Street, St. Paul, MN 55101-3885 USA.

ISBN-13: 978-0-7603-2218-5
ISBN-10: 0-7603-2218-X

Editors: Steve Gansen and Lindsay Hitch
Designer: Kally Lane

Printed in China

On the front cover:
The world's largest airliner in at its public debut 'Reveal' ceremony in Toulouse, France on January 18, 2005. *Mark Wagner*

On the frontispiece:
At air shows around the world, models of the A3XX and 747-500X/600X vied for the attention of the attendees wandering the exhibit halls. *Mark Wagner*

On the title page:
The cross section of the A380 allowed up to 25 containers to be loaded into the upper deck, 33 in the main deck, and 13 in the lower deck. Total available volume, including bulk cargo in the lower aft hold, was a remarkable 1,240 cubic yards. *Mark Wagner*

On the back cover:
Some idea of the structural scale of the A380 can be glimpsed in this impressive view of the completed fuselage center section 15/21 of MSN006 at Saint-Nazaire, France. Measuring just over 28 feet tall and 23 feet, 5 inches wide at its widest point, the lower part of the section is also configured with support struts for the belly fairing that is attached during final assembly in Toulouse. *Mark Wagner*

With the bulk of the early flight test program responsibilities on its shoulders, MSN001 was expected to conduct about 600 hours of the planned 2,100-hour test effort for the Trent 900-powered A380. This program would also involve three other aircraft: MSN002, 004, and 007. *Mark Wagner*

MBI Publishing Company would like to thank Airbus for providing images from the following:

exm/H. Goussé; P. Masclet: pages 8, 32, 57, 67 (upper), 92 (upper right), 92 (lower), 93 (upper), 93 (lower), 94, 100 (upper), 101 (lower), 102 (lower), 103, 120 (center), 135 (lower), 152 (lower)

i3M: 38, 72, 74 (lower), 77 (upper), 77 (lower), 144 (upper)

TABLE OF CONTENTS

ACKNOWLEDGMENTS

We are deeply indebted to the countless Airbus employees, past and present, who helped bring this project to life. For recounting the highlights of the design, engineering, and marketing story, we thank Jean Roeder, Jerome Pora, Frank Ogilvie, Colin Stuart, and Wolf-Dieter Wissel. For opening doors and helping us along the way, we thank Barbara Kracht and her fine communications team. In particular, thanks to David Velupillai, Debra Batson, Daniel Bled, Rolf Brandt, Mark Challoner, Nadine Coedel, Laetitia Combes, Ann De-Crozals, Yannick Delamarre, Daphne Dewachter, Francois Fournier, Fabian Guerrero, Mathilde Graux, Jose Luis Hormigos, Jean Michel Janniere, Georges Lecoq, Francoise Maenhaut, Karen Mitchell, Sylvia Philp, Tore Prang, Fabienne Royet, Caroline Tabbernee, and Suzane Zlaket. Also to Dietmar Plath for his desktop model and to Rick Kennedy, Deb Case, Jim Stump, and Mark Sullivan of the GeneralElectric/Pratt and Whitney Engine Alliance. Also Janina Cross, Robert Nuttall, Alistair Coast Smith, Andrew Siddons, and Martin Johnson of Rolls-Royce. We would like to thank Mary Kane and Tom Lubbesmeyer of Boeing, as well as Caroline Harris of Smiths Industries, Thomas Niepel, Martin Butler of Goodrich, Lori Krans of Hamilton Sundstrand, and Erich Wagner. For help with research, we thank Rob Grundy, Stuart Buchan, and Joe Wollner, and to Graham Warwick for help with proofreading. Thanks also to colleagues and friends at *Flight International*, including Andrew Doyle, Max Kingsley Jones, Murdo Morrison, Chris Thornton, and Paul Gladman. For patience, help, and understanding, our gratitude goes to Stephanie Day and Anna Ravelo, as well as to Henry Wagner; Tom and Greg Norris; Christopher, Daniel, and Lia Ravelo. Last, but not least, we extend our gratitude to Scott Stickland at aviation-images.com and a special thanks to Steve Gansen and Lindsay Hitch at MBI Publishing Company.

PROLOGUE

Sowing the Seeds of a Superjumbo

In the warm summer of 1988, a small group of advanced project engineers in Airbus Industrie's Toulouse headquarters gathered around a table to study rough sketches of something few of them really believed would ever be built.

It was a giant aircraft capable of carrying more than 800 passengers—an unprecedented behemoth of a jetliner that would one day challenge the mighty Boeing 747, the latest -400 version of which had just started flight tests in the United States. This group of engineers specialized in future projects, and crazy ideas were their bread and butter; but until then none of them had seen proposals for anything quite so large, so bold, so audacious, and so top secret.

Only this small group, working for the New Product Development and Technology branch of Airbus, knew of the project, dubbed the ultra-high-capacity aircraft (UHCA). At this stage, the project's existence was totally unknown to the rest of the consortium, including the leadership of Airbus.

To Jean Roeder, the group's leader and brilliant engineer behind the concept of the shared wing on the A330 and A340, the UHCA was something that Airbus simply had to do. Boeing had reaped the benefits of a full family of airliners for more than two decades and had enjoyed its megajet monopoly for too long. If Airbus Industrie was to become a real global player, Roeder argued that the 747 monopoly would have to end. "Airbus was making efforts at this time to get 30 percent of the market, and we thought that this just would not be possible in the long term if we did not get a complete set of aircraft in our program." said Roeder, senior vice president of product development and technology. "It was my job to look at what we needed to do."

Roeder acknowledged there were other, more selfish, motivations. "We badly needed the design work. All the big programs at the time had just been completed. In addition, within Europe we urgently needed a new technology vehicle. We had all the technology that was available at the time, most of it going into the aircraft on the line, and there wasn't much left up our sleeves."

The small group in the Technical Directorate pushed the idea around for a few months. "We asked ourselves, is it possible? Does it make sense? And only after we had convinced ourselves there was something here that could be done, we started to make a wider effort," said Roeder, who had first come from Munich in the early days of Airbus to help work on the cross section of the very first A300.

Tentatively at first, Roeder began making discrete sanity calls to colleagues. Sid Swadling, Airbus chief engineer at British Aerospace (BAe) Filton, told him that the major new component would be the wing. "It was clear that whatever we decided to do, it would be a BAe wing. So when I asked what we should be working on next, to my surprise he said we ought to be doing something the size of the 747, and I already had that in my pocket and I hadn't dared say a thing."

Encouraged by the reactions they received, the team pressed on and, in October 1988, Roeder asked for a lunchtime

Seventeen years after it first dared to dream the seemingly impossible, Airbus successfully flew the world's first superjumbo. The first A380-800 performs a triumphant flyby over the main runway at Toulouse toward the end of its maiden flight on April 27, 2005.
Mark Wagner

Jean Roeder, the exceptional engineer behind the common design philosophy of the A330 and A340, came up with the plan to use a similar concept to go even further—into the realm of the superjumbo. Although Roeder's original plan did not come to fruition, it planted the seed from which the A3XX and later the A380 would grow. *Airbus*

meeting to discuss future projects with Airbus president Jean Pierson and chief operating officer Herbert Flosdorff. The three met at the Airbus corporate restaurant, a five-star establishment in its own right, and discussed the issues. Pierson asked: "Well, Jean, what are you going to do next?"

"I reached into a plastic bag that I had brought into the meeting with me, and pulled out a model we had had made up and put it on the table. He was clearly surprised; he did not expect anything that big," said Roeder, laughing at the memory.

Pierson looked at Roeder's model and instantly saw the possibilities. But he also saw risks. What if word got out before Airbus was ready? What if a competitor, or even one of the partners themselves, decided to take the initiative away from Airbus before the project could be properly assessed? "Pierson was very, very careful, and he was right. If you start going out with something like this too early, even with your partners, you are risking failure. It had to be done right, and if we were going to propose something new, the partners would all have to go and find the money," said Roeder.

The idea would remain a secret for another two years while Airbus carefully began its UHCA work. But it would take more than a small model and a bit of market research to launch a project of this scale. What economic and societal forces were at play to make Airbus believe that a market could exist for an aircraft bigger than the 747?

Changing Worlds

In 1988, news of a changing world frequently dominated lunchtime talk in the Airbus dining room. At the top of the agenda for discussion was the approaching end of the Cold War—the unremitting stand-off between East and West that had gripped the world for four decades. Under the benign influence of the recently elected Communist party general secretary Mikhail Gorbachev, the late 1980s had seen the Soviet Union embark on the twin paths of *perestroika*, or restructuring, and the equally painful process of *glasnost*, or openness.

By 1989, with Gorbachev's appointment as president of the Soviet Union, the radical reforms in the U.S.S.R. became a prelude to the equally sudden meltdown of the Communist regimes throughout eastern Europe. The astounding spectacle of the Berlin Wall being pulled, pushed, and bulldozed out of existence in November 1989 appeared to be a bellwether of a new epoch of global freedom and peaceful coexistence.

To aircraft manufacturers and airlines, these events heralded the potential for travel and trade on an unprecedented scale. Business flourished while air passenger traffic climbed at or above a worldwide annual average of 5 percent, with some 1.2 billion travelers making a journey by air that year. For reassurance, Airbus needed to look no further than the Asia-Pacific market, where the relentless expansion of the Tiger economies of the region fueled double-digit surges in passenger air traffic. By the end of the 1980s, the Asia-Pacific region already accounted for more than 21 percent of the world's gross domestic product (GDP), a 50 percent increase since 1970, and was forecast to grow to about 27 percent by 2000. Since GDP is generally the single most important variable when predicting air traffic volume, planners recognized the clear signal that Asian-based airlines and their international competitors would be in line for expansion.

It didn't take a rocket scientist to see that more people traveling created a demand for more aircraft. But more aircraft also meant more congestion, and pundits on both sides of the Atlantic turned their attention to predicting how this would affect the size of future aircraft. Would runway and airspace capacity limits dictate a move to larger and larger aircraft, or would infrastructure improvements and more efficient medium-sized aircraft be better ways to meet the rising demand?

This was the pivotal $12 billion question that would launch the race for the next-generation superjumbo, and that would ultimately drive a philosophical wedge between Airbus and Boeing for more than a decade.

In Asia, at least, the omens clearly warned of congestion to come, and statistics indicated the devastating possibility of virtual gridlock in Hong Kong, Taiwan, and Japan, in particular. Figures showed that weekly aircraft arrivals and departures at the top 10 major airports in the

Although it was originally the year-on-year traffic growth of the "Tiger" economies throughout Asia that sparked the ultra-high-capacity aircraft (UHCA) development race of the 1990s, the Japanese carriers remained cautious observers of the A380 program as it entered flight tests in 2005. Here, the prototype, with gear stowed, is seen heading back to Toulouse to resume flight tests after taking part in the Paris Air Show that year.

region jumped from 6,500 in 1971 to 10,000 in 1980, and to 16,600 in 1989. The trend indicated that total arrivals and departures would reach 27,000 per week by 1999, or an average increase of 60 percent in airport congestion.

For the moment, however, the big divide was still ahead, and Airbus and Boeing appeared to be reading the same script. In its 1990 forecast, Boeing predicted a steady increase in average aircraft size from fewer than 190 seats to almost 230 seats in 2005. While this may not seem like a significant difference, remember this was the average, making it a sure sign that there would be a need for more aircraft as large as, or larger than, the 747.

Boeing's 747 sales figures also supported the need for more large jets, further fueling Roeder's argument for an Airbus counterattack. From the end of 1985, when Boeing announced the launch of the higher-capacity -400 model, through 1990, Boeing had picked up a staggering 382 new 747 orders—130 of them in 1990 alone!

Overall, Boeing predicted a demand for about 2,500 airliners with more than 350 seats between 1990 and 2005, while the closest equivalent predictions from Airbus saw a need for 2,800 aircraft between 300 and 500 seats in the period from 1990 to 2009. In the Asia-Pacific region alone, the consensus showed that the long-range fleet of aircraft with more than 350 seats would rise from 250 in 1990 to 920 by 2005. Even McDonnell Douglas, still at this stage a powerful force in air transport, was considering new ventures to probe the larger aircraft market with new derivatives of its recently launched MD-11 trijet.

While their predictions differed slightly, Airbus, Boeing, and McDonnell Douglas all agreed that the big battleground was not necessarily in the jumbo category, but rather in the midsize market, where a new range of aircraft was competing to replace fleets of McDonnell Douglas DC-10s and Lockheed L-1011 TriStar wide-bodied trijets. Beyond this was a potential market of more than 2,000 more aircraft to fill the inevitable demand for growth in mid- and long-range routes.

Although no one could have predicted it at the time, the race to fill this market would have far-reaching effects that would forever change the face of commercial aviation. Not only would the race contribute to the eventual disappearance of one of the most famous company names in the business, it would also establish the basis from which Airbus would launch its pivotal assault on the superjumbo market.

INTRODUCTION

Poised for takeoff on that hot morning in April 2005, the Airbus A380 had the purposeful, powerful presence of a giant predatory bird. With its enormous gulled wings; imperiously tall tail; and broad, domed forepeak, it looked ready to take on the world, champion its supporters, and silence its critics. And there have been plenty of both. No civil airliner since the supersonic Concorde has aroused such passion, such controversy, and such fascination.

To friend and foe alike, all agree it is a phenomenal engineering achievement. To some, the superjumbo is a magnificent cruise liner of the skies with unprecedented money-making potential. To others, it is a huge white elephant with questionable economics and a slim chance of success.

To a confident Airbus and the thousands of awestruck workers who cheered it into that cloudless sky over Toulouse, it means so much more. Under the broad wings of this incredible project, the European company has been reborn as a single corporate entity—transformed from a loose consortium into a new, more dynamic force to challenge its worthy adversary Boeing in every market sector.

The A380, which was designed to bring people together on a scale never before seen, had touched thousands of lives before it even flew. The very act of creating the superjumbo has forged a globe-spanning network of more than 100 international suppliers and partners in more than 20 countries. The superjumbo infrastructure, therefore, matches the industrial scale and sophistication of a space program.

And scale and space is what the A380 is all about. The aircraft is almost as large as the list of superlatives frequently used to describe it. The first airliner designed to carry almost 900 passengers in its baseline version, it has the most spacious interior of any jetliner ever built, the biggest wings, and the greatest overall engine thrust. Its double-deck load, hopes Airbus, will help relieve congestion at airports by taking up less space than the two airliners it can replace. In that sense, it is also the "greenest" long haul airliner yet developed, burning less than 1 gallon of fuel per passenger over 95 miles, a fuel consumption comparable with a small turbo-diesel family car.

As these words were written, the age of the superjumbo was in its infancy, flight tests were underway and deliveries about to begin.

This book, therefore, tells the story of where the A380 has come from, how it was designed and built, and gives a guide as to where it is going in the future. Time, of course, will reveal the true destiny of the superjumbo. Given the skill, spirit, commitment, and passion of all those involved in the birth of this remarkable aircraft, however, the signs are that the A380 will be the flagship of the twenty-first century and take its place as one of the greatest aircraft ever made.

–Guy Norris and Mark Wagner, July 2005

The A380 was the first large Airbus model to have a fuselage wider than the 18-foot-6-inch-diameter cross section body originally conceived for the first product, the A300B. Developed as the fir
so spacious at the time that early operators such as Air France actively encouraged passengers to bring luggage on board rather than check it in for transport in the baggage hold! Here the per
containing two LD-3 cargo containers side-by-side below the main deck, is shown to good effect as an early Air France A300B4 taxies at London Heathrow. *Mark Wagner*

1

Back to the Roots

As Jean Roeder was presenting his plans for the future, development work was under-way on the Airbus A330 and A340, the largest airliners yet designed in Europe. They, in turn, traced their ancestry directly back 20 years to the first Airbus product, the A300. Developed as the world's first wide-bodied twinjet, the A300 was the product of a European study into a new "air bus" to link major hubs such as London and Paris.

The study was the work of an Anglo-French government working group that encapsulated its findings in a 1965 report, "Outline Specification for the High-Capacity Short-Haul Aircraft." This formed the DNA for what was to become Airbus Industrie, the French-based European consortium formally established in December 1970 to challenge the dominance of American commercial jet makers.

Although it was a notable engineering achievement, the A300 failed to impress many of the world's airlines when it first flew in October 1972. With very slow sales, the big twin limped almost unnoticed through the early 1970s. The giant U.S. aircraft manufacturers scoffed at it, and the global recession that the oil crisis in the Middle East sparked severely hampered it. These were dangerously vulnerable years for Airbus, which held onto life by a thread, selling only a single aircraft in 1976 and producing only one aircraft per month.

But airlines that were forced to adjust to higher fuel prices in the late 1970s gradually recognized the economic appeal of a wide-body twin. The basic concept of a large twin, ironically, had come from an early American Airlines specification, and it was a U.S.-based carrier, Eastern Airlines, that provided the sales breakthrough. The April 1978 order for 23 A300B4s by Eastern, the first North American customer for Airbus, instantly gave the

e-body twin in the world, the cabin seemed
circular fuselage cross section, neatly

fledgling manufacturer a new measure of credibility that it has kept to this day. It's interesting to note that the original American specification also led directly to the birth of the DC-10 and the L-1011—both trijets. Eventually, in 1987, American Airlines did order a fleet of A300-600Rs, which served it well into the twenty-first century.

Interim developments of the A300, including the A310 and the A300-600, were followed in 1980 by an expansion into the single-aisle, short-haul market with the A320. The diversification helped strengthen the industrial base of Airbus at a grassroots level beyond Europe, and just as importantly established the manufacturer's reputation across a much broader range of airlines and operators.

Airbus based all its wide-body designs on the same 18-foot, 6-inch diameter fuselage cross section of the first A300. The fuselage was perfectly circular and provided enough width to accommodate two LD3 containers (the industry standard for cargo shipping) to be housed side-by-side in the lower cargo hold.

Satisfied with the logic of its cross section, which has frequently been identified as the most important specification in any new passenger aircraft design, Airbus always intended to stick with this platform for future higher-capacity designs.

Two of these original projects were designated A300B9 and A300B11. After the A320 launch, they were renamed TA9 and TA11, respectively, to indicate that they were twin-aisle projects. The TA9 was essentially a stretched A300 with more powerful engines for medium stage lengths, while the TA11 was to be the first Airbus design powered by four engines for long-haul routes. Even at this stage, however, Airbus did not presume to tread on the toes of Boeing and invade the sacred territory of the 747. The TA11 was simply aimed at replacing the 707 and DC-8 on long, thin routes which, although covering vast distances, were not sufficiently busy to fill an aircraft the size of the 747. Studies into the TA9 and TA11 continued into the 1980s under the leadership of Jean Pierson, but the big question of which one Airbus should launch remained.

The breakthrough, in terms of affordability, came when Roeder, then Airbus chief engineer, hit upon the idea of using the same wing for both designs. The aircraft already shared common fuselages, systems, flight decks, and tails, so the idea of using essentially the same wing became even more appealing to the consortium. Pierson would later recall the debate that raged within Airbus: "Some people said we should launch a twin, others a quad. Finally, the engineers promised they could do both with a common airframe for half a billion less. So I said, 'Let's go!'"

Adam Brown, who was vice president for strategic planning during the early years of the A330/A340 and later the A3XX/A380 programs, remembered that Roeder and his team were "able to create a common wing structure, with the quad's outboard engines providing bending relief to counteract the increased weights of the long-range model. The cost savings this presented enabled us to do both aircraft. The idea was really a piece of brilliant insight."

Following an Airbus supervisory board meeting in Munich in January 1986, the designations of the TA9 and TA11 officially became the A330 and A340, respectively. Originally, Airbus intended to launch the four-engine TA11 first, because it was attracting the most immediate interest from airlines. So the plan was to call the TA11 the A330, and the twin-engine TA9 the A340. However, as Brown recalled: "Our salesman came back and said that airlines would never get their brains around a twin having a four in its name and the quad not, so we reversed the designations."

The pair was finally launched on the eve of the 1987 Paris Air Show, with two versions of the A340 being offered: a 260-seat -200 and a 295-seat -300. At the time, only one version of the A330 was available, the 295-seat -300. The A340 entered service with Lufthansa in March 1993, followed by the A330 with Air Inter in 1994. A later, shorter version of the A330, the 250-seat -200, was subsequently developed and entered service in 1998. The later variant of the twin would prove to be one of the most popular members of the family, eventually outselling Boeing's 767.

Airbus was already trying to figure out how to get more passengers into the A340 as it glimpsed the possibilities of taking a slice—but only a slice—of the Classic 747 replacement market. The epithet Classic had not yet come into vogue, but even by the late 1980s it was obvious that the improvements in the newly developed 747-400 would spark an eventual replacement race for the older generation 747-100, -200, and -300 versions.

In September 1989, even before assembly of the first 295-passenger A340-300 had begun, Airbus revealed studies of a double-deck modification that would seat up to 60 passengers in a converted forward belly hold.

The move was designed to counter the MD-11 rather than take on the 747, but it got Airbus planners thinking and soon morphed into a more ambitious stretch derivative with greater market appeal dubbed the A340-400X. Almost immediately, however, the study ran into trouble because of the limited power of the incumbent CFM56 engines.

The -400X plan involved stretching the fuselage by 20 feet, 7 inches, which would provide capacity for 340 passengers in three classes. But without changing engines and wing design, the range capability was hopelessly penalized by about 1,500 nautical miles compared to the baseline A340-300, rendering the

Spreading its wings into the narrow-body business, Airbus developed the A320 as the world's first commercial transport with a digital fly-by-wire (FBW) flight control system. (The Anglo-French Concorde was fitted with an analogue system.) Based on earlier developments first used on the A310 and proven on an A300 demonstrator, the system provides hazard protection throughout the flight and was further developed for the much larger A330/340 and A380. The A320 family quickly became a best seller, with more than 3,500 ordered and almost 2,500 delivered by late 2005. Here an early-model British Airways A320-100, originally ordered by long-defunct British Caledonian and distinguished by its lack of winglets, is pictured on approach to London Heathrow during a late winter afternoon in 2001.
Mark Wagner

nautical miles. At 247 feet, 1 inch, in length, the A340-600 became the longest airliner ever built, while the A340-500, at 222 feet, 7 inches, became the longest range airliner ever built. From the moment these aircraft entered service in 2002, both helped confirm beyond doubt the credibility of Airbus in the long-haul jetliner market, while at the same time securing a precious foothold on the virtually untapped ultra-long nonstop routes that beckoned between the United States and Asia.

Studies Begin

It was the inherent flexibility of the basic A340 fuselage that Roeder seized on for the new UHCA project in late 1988. "The purpose was to try and do something at the lowest possible cost by using as much as we could from the existing products. When I presented the original project to Pierson, it was all based on what we could afford."

Wolf-Dieter Wissel, who Roeder appointed to lead the UHCA study project and who would ultimately become the director of configuration integration for the A380, said: "It all came from first ideas on a piece of paper, almost on the back of an envelope, if you like. To be honest, it was all a bit like a dream, there was nothing available from which to start. But one of Roeder's brilliant ideas was to use the A340 design elements to create this horizontal double-bubble [HDB] concept. We took the A340 fuselage and sort of stretched the fuselage laterally and put the A340 wings on it and used slightly larger versions of the HTP [horizontal tailplane] and both vertical tails."

The bizarre-looking concept was sized to be about 20 percent larger than the 747-400, and could therefore seat up to 517 in a three-class configuration. A flight deck was perched cupola-style atop the fuselage. The Airbus technical director at the time, Bernard Ziegler, was also keen to emphasize the possibilities of a clean-sheet design. "We've got to think about a wider fuselage. We get no lift at all from the fuselage today," he said when details of the design began to emerge.

Pierson and Flosdorff had given Roeder the go-ahead to continue with studies, and the Airbus supervisory board gave its official approval for further evaluations after Roeder's first formal presentation to them in June 1990. With that approval, Airbus decided to gingerly put its toe in the market with the concept at the 1990 Farnborough Air Show that time between 2003 and 2005. Airbus set a goal of having direct operating costs that were at least 15 percent

-400X a dud before it even got off the drawing board. But the -400X exercise was not a wasted effort.

Airbus had seen a vision of the future and was intrigued by the possibilities of this emerging market opportunity, so it canvassed engine manufacturers for a larger powerplant for its stretched A340. In 1991, Airbus Engineering Vice President Bernard Ziegler prophesied: "One day, for sure, we'll have new-generation engines for this aircraft."

In the end, it took a torturous six years of negotiation, redesign, indecision, market uncertainty, and posturing before the project finally emerged as a qualified challenger to the Classic 747. By now it had again evolved, this time into a two-member family renamed the A340-500 and -600. In another break with tradition for Airbus, which had used General Electric and Pratt & Whitney engines for all its widebodies up to the A330, it signed a virtually exclusive deal with British manufacturer Rolls-Royce for the Trent 500 engine.

The new A340 design, coupled with a larger wing and more powerful engines, could carry 378 passengers and their luggage across ranges of up to 7,300 nautical miles, or right in the middle of the Classic 747 replacement frame. Furthermore, by trading airframe weight for range, the shorter -500 sibling could carry 313 passengers over the great distance of 8,300

Adaptability and innovation were hallmarks of the Airbus heritage, largely driven by the need to do more with less. The use of a common wing on both the twin-engined A330 and the four-engined A340 was a key enabler to making the entire project affordable. The outboard engine on the A340 is located adjacent to the gap between the outer flap section and the inboard edge of the aileron, and provides wing bending relief moment to the structure of the longer-range variants. The inboard engine is sited at the same location as the engine on the A330, pictured here on the -200 demonstrator during a flying display at the 2000 Farnborough Air Show. Externally, the only difference between the two wings is a split between the fourth and fifth leading edge slat on the A340 wing. *Mark Wagner*

lower than the operating costs of the 747-400, though Jean Pierson told Flight International in May 1991 that the development would take account of "the improvements they [Boeing] will make to the 747 by the year 2000 . . . our obligation is to offer something to the market that is far better than that."

With so much at stake, and with the need to focus on specific new support technologies for a UHCA, Airbus and its four partners launched a joint technology program. This new partnership was formed under the auspices of the European 3E (environment, economy, energy) technology effort originally organized by Airbus, its partners, and the European governments in the late 1980s to coordinate and rationalize research efforts.

In this case, the new initiative was directed at defining three new technology demonstration platforms for the single-aisle A320-size class, one for the A340-size category, and one in the 500-seat arena.

This novel approach ensured that Airbus would utilize the best ideas and technologies from throughout Europe by organizing four pre-project teams from its partners—Aerospatiale, Deutsche Aerospace (DASA), British Aerospace, and Construcciones Aeronáuticas, SA (CASA). The plan directed the four teams to effectively compete with different designs to be presented to the Airbus supervisory board by early

17

Designing the A340, the consortium's first four-engined model, taught Airbus valuable lessons that would be used to good effect when developing the structural and systems redundancy of the A380. It also shared a common cockpit with the A330 and helped establish the principle of crew cross-qualification, which enabled pilots to quickly transition not only between the big twin and its quad sister ship, but also between these larger aircraft and the A320. Total orders for the CFM International CFM56-5C-powered A340-200/300 family topped 240 by mid-2005. *Mark Wagner*

A bigger wing and more powerful Rolls-Royce Trent 500 turbofans rejuvenated the A340 and, with the 380-passenger -600 version in particular, gave Airbus the ability to take on the 747 for the first time. The development allowed the model to penetrate two Boeing strongholds—ultra-long range and high capacity—though the shorter bodied -500 faced massive competitive pressure from the twin-engined 777-200LR. With combined orders of about 140 by mid-2005, the duo spearheaded the Airbus attack on the upper end of the "fragmented" point-to-point market. *Mark Wagner*

1992. The board would then select one or two of the most competitive designs, and if none were sufficiently cost-competitive with the 747 they would have to go back to the drawing board. "We were expecting we would need new technology to meet the range and weight targets. We knew it could not be done using the existing technology of those days; that was clearly understood," said Wissel.

Airbus remained confident, however, that one or more of the teams would come up with a world-beater, or at least a design that could be merged with features of the other contestants and possibly even those of the in-house concepts. This would then allow the concept to be formally adopted in 1993 in preparation for a launch in 1996 or 1997. At this stage, Airbus planned to begin searching for risk-sharing partners and estimated that the overall development cost would be in the $4 to $5 billion range—an enormous amount of money that would eventually form less than half of the new airliner's final cost.

Airbus' first publicly revealed UHCA concept was an unusually configured aircraft with a wide fuselage made up of two A340 fuselages melded side by side. The idea was the brainchild of Roeder, who believed the use of existing A340 components, including wings, tails, and other systems, would be the only way to afford to attempt such an ambitious project. The concept got as far as the wind tunnel stage but did not produce encouraging results. *Airbus*

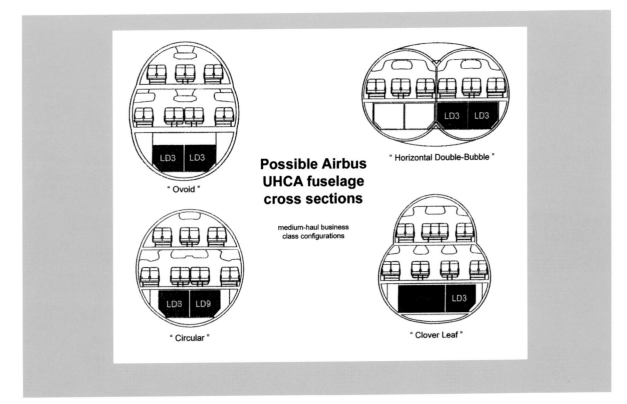

Possible Airbus UHCA fuselage cross sections

"Ovoid"

"Horizontal Double-Bubble"

medium-haul business class configurations

"Circular"

"Clover Leaf"

Personally thanked by French President Jacques Chirac for his decisive role in launching the A380, former Airbus President Jean Pierson is pictured during the early 1990s at the beginning of the UHCA odyssey. His aim from the start was to take the 747 head-on, and more particularly any upgraded variant. "Our obligation," he said, "is to offer something to the market that is far better than that." *Mark Wagner*

Nearly everyone in the airliner industry agrees that the most important design decision in the history of any jetliner is the cross section. With no option but to go for a clean-sheet configuration, Airbus studied everything from a giant circular section, which limited the upper deck options, to a "clover leaf" design that provided optimum space but was less aerodynamically and structurally efficient. Top right is the famous A340-derived horizontal double-bubble section, while the "ovoid" cross section finally adopted is pictured top left. *Airbus*

Reacting to the booming traffic growth across the Pacific in the late 1980s and early 1990s, United issued a broad specification to Boeing in 1991 for a UHCA aircraft dubbed the N650. It establish and pushed Boeing's studies up in size well beyond the 415-seat 747-400. The larger size category of the United spec would later drive an insurmountable wedge between Boeing and the Europ commercial transport (VLCT) joint studies. *Mark Wagner*

2

Let the
Battle Commence

Airbus had been making all the noise about new-generation jumbos, but that was about to change. In June 1991, just before the Paris Air Show, it was revealed that United Airlines chairman Stephen Wolf had asked Boeing to study United's requirement for a 650-seat transpacific aircraft. Dubbed the N650, the requirement galvanized Boeing into action and triggered a bizarre series of events, the effects of which forever altered the face of civil aviation, and which are still being felt today.

Boeing took United's request very seriously despite the fact that only 17 months earlier it had launched the 777 on the back of a launch order from the massive Chicago-based carrier. Within a few days of United's request, Boeing began to sketch a series of three main concepts: a stretched 747, a full double-deck variant of the 747, and a clean-sheet design. The first details of Boeing's response came at the Paris Air Show, where the company's executive vice president, Phil Condit, said: "We fully intend to compete in that double-deck version market."

Boeing also appointed a former marketing vice president, John Hayhurst, as vice president for large aircraft development. To Hayhurst, the writing was on the wall for a new-generation jumbo, particularly when Boeing had forecast in 1991 that 54 percent of the value of the commercial market up to 2005, or roughly $334 billion, was for 350-seaters and upward. "We believe we can fulfill that by a combination of 747- and 777-sized aircraft as well as a requirement for an aircraft larger than the 747-400," said Hayhurst. "We have had a number of product developments aimed at this, ranging from stretches of the 747-400 to all-new aircraft. What we're doing is bringing together all the efforts we've had up to now and focusing them to find out what the market needs are for this segment

and then to design it." The simplest option, the proposed 747 stretch, was slightly larger than the -400, a tried-and-tested Boeing formula used on everything from the 707 onward.

The United and Boeing move had a sudden impact on Airbus, which announced an accelerated schedule for its jumbo effort, calling for launch in 1995 and entry into service some time after 2000. As if taken up with this greater sense of urgency, Airbus shareholder Deutsche Aerospace (DASA) also unveiled details of its initial proposals to meet the new jumbo requirements. Its leviathan was a conventional configuration called the A2000. Not unlike the final Airbus superjumbo in overall configuration, it measured 255 feet in length, with a massive wingspan of 262 feet. It had an overall height of 75 feet, a wing area of 8,180 square feet, and a maximum takeoff weight of 1.16 million pounds. The A2000 was designed to seat 615 passengers on three decks, with economy passengers on the upper deck, business travelers on the main deck, and first-class passengers, for whom beds would be available, on the lower deck.

DASA suggested a suite of advanced-technology features for its configuration that would help achieve a 15 percent fuel burn improvement over the 747-400, a target that would continue to be a benchmark for the eventual Airbus project. These features included a fly-by-wire flight-control system to help offset weight by creating a smaller empennage. DASA

also proposed the possible use of laminar-flow control on the wing and tail, but it ruled out the use of carbon-fiber composites in the primary structure of the wing.

DASA also recognized that such a huge aircraft would present a psychological barrier to overall acceptance but added that it would be built nonetheless. The company's executive vice president for design and technology, Professor Uwe Ganzer, said at the time: "We're seeing such an increase in traffic that it is inevitable."

Boeing, driven largely by the inspiration of United, tentatively saw a similar vision. Speaking in September 1991 at the U.K. Institution of Civil Engineers, Boeing Product Strategy Analysis Manager Richard Bateman said that a 600-seater could take a large chunk of a market forecast to be worth some $617 billion through 2005. Bateman painted a picture of an all-new design that used four 777-size engines and had a fuselage cross section of 27 feet, 9 inches, in diameter. This would allow up to 12-abreast seating on the main deck and up to 8 abreast on the upper deck, while providing sufficient capacity for up to three LD3 containers on the lower deck.

The wingspan was an impressive 259 feet, but with folding wingtips to enable it to fit into existing 747-400 gates. Although approximately 18 feet shorter in length than the A2000, the new design was almost exactly the same height and had an array of upper and main deck doors for loading and unloading.

The concept, loosely dubbed the 787, "could be in service by the end of the century if the market wants it," said Bateman.

But did it? United, which scheduled two 747-400 departures within 10 minutes of each other on the New York–Tokyo route, obviously saw a need, but what about everyone else? The only way to get the answers was to ask the airlines, and that is precisely what Airbus and Boeing began to do as 1991 came to a close.

Teams from both manufacturers headed to the headquarters of the world's biggest airlines, the bulk of them in the Asia-Pacific region. Airbus marketers visited about a dozen carriers, hoping to present their findings to the four special project teams set up to study the UHCA. Speaking in Singapore that same hectic September, Airbus Marketing Vice President David Jennings said: "We are at the stage where we think it is technically feasible. We think that Airbus could produce such an aircraft, and we are testing some of our assumptions about the market."

Boeing visited Qantas Airways in Australia and learned that the carrier was really more desperate for a shorter-term 747 stretch solution. But after hearing encouraging news at an operators conference in Hawaii, Boeing set up a customer advisory committee like it had for the 767-X, which led to the 777. The committee was comprised of prospective customers that included the usual suspects, namely United; British Airways; Qantas; and the two key Japanese jumbo operators, Japan Air Lines (JAL) and All Nippon Airways (ANA), as well as Cathay Pacific Airways and Thai Airways International.

Speaking in South Korea after the November 1991 handover of the first 747-400 to Asiana, a new Seoul-based airline, Boeing's Everett division vice president, James Johnson, said: "The decision must be made for a stretch of the 747-400 or a new aircraft or both—we're actually considering both. There is active interest in a new, large 650- to 680-seat airplane, and there are a number of customers who'd like us to do it real soon."

Using 777 technologies, Johnson believed that a new design was probably the best option. "We could go to a circular double-deck cross section, which is lighter and more efficient and which obviates the cargo capability," he added. Rather more surprising was news that the new giant, should it go ahead, would probably not be built in Everett—the traditional manufacturing site of all Boeing wide-bodies. The reasons given were site congestion plus the increasing specter of high taxes in Washington state. In addition,

Johnson said that the effort would "probably be financed by ourselves, with a sort of co-manufacturing arrangement with someone like the Japanese on the 777, though not necessarily the Japanese."

At the same Asiana delivery meeting was Boeing's vice president for international sales, James Chorlton, who, like his equals within Airbus, appeared keenly aware of the massive market opportunities of the Asia-Pacific region. "This is big aircraft country. For people like JAL, ANA, and Thai, the bigger the airplane the better. They keep saying: 'Are you going to build it, and when, and how big?'" Chorlton also fired from the hip when it came to China and its prospects. "China's traffic is growing by twenty percent a year internally and ten to twelve percent internationally. They have a whole warehouse of Russian junk that has to be done away with, and it's a big market for aircraft. China Southeast wants the biggest airplanes we can build."

Boeing's challenge—and a problem that Airbus did not have—was whether it should take advantage of the well-established 747 family—and everything that meant in terms of commonality, manufacturing experience, and infrastructure—or whether it should go for an all-new design. The 747-derivative option was not necessarily the easiest, but it was the cheapest. The two 747 studies included a 23-foot, 4-inch stretch that would add 84 seats, taking typical three-class seating to 484, and a more radical modification that extended the hump of the upper deck aft along the entire length of the main-deck cabin. But, as with any derivatives, both 747s suffered from being sub-optimized designs. Range was the big issue, with the stretch plane being capable of only 80 percent of the -400's range, while the upper-deck stretch would only have 73 percent of the range.

China's unbelievable economic boom was still slowly building when this sleepy parochial scene was captured at Xian Airport in 1986. The 1950s vintage Ilyushin IL-14 in the foreground was still in regular front-line passenger service, while the Tupolev Tu-154M was brand new, having just been delivered from the then-Soviet Union. Even at this early stage, the replacement market was beckoning and, as Boeing's senior international sales supremo James Chorlton pointed out: "They have a whole warehouse of Russian junk that has to be done away with, and it's a big market for aircraft." Chinese Premier Zhou Enlai obviously disagreed with Chorlton's assessment of the IL-14 (or "Crate," to use its NATO code name), as he used one as his personal transport. The aircraft is preserved today in a museum in Tianjin. *Mark Wagner*

A Surprise Challenger

But it was neither Airbus nor Boeing that emerged first with a firm new double-decker design, it was—to the shock of the industry—the Douglas Aircraft Division of the McDonnell Douglas Corporation (MDC). The Long Beach, California–based manufacturer had not even registered on the radar screen as far as the UHCA race was concerned, but had been busy for several years attempting to bolster its flagging product line with a stretched derivative of the MD-11, dubbed the MD-12X. In early 1992, however, the airlines that were closely involved with the MD-12X studies began pressing for a more efficient four-engine design with greater growth potential.

The sudden abandonment of Douglas's familiar trijet heritage took everyone by surprise, especially Airbus and Boeing, which looked on with curiosity at the proposed new design. Remarkably, given the design heritage of the MD-11 from the DC-10 and the smaller MD-80/90 twins from the DC-9, the revised MD-12X would have represented the first all-new commercial transport to be designed by Douglas since it started formal development work on the DC-10 in 1968!

The lack of investment by St. Louis–based McDonnell Douglas in its Long Beach commercial airplane division over the years had resulted in a disjointed product lineup with yawning gaps. While Boeing, and later Airbus, had developed complete families covering all the capacities from 100 seats up, Douglas was dependent on its mid-market MD-80/90 and larger-capacity MD-11 for business, and was left vulnerable to the ups and downs of the market.

Douglas had recognized its predicament for years, becoming acutely aware of the problem in the late 1980s when it began doing its sums over the estimated $1 billion cost of developing a new supercritical wing for the stretched MD-11. It had even held discussions with Airbus over the faint chance of using a derivative of the A330/A340 wing, and talks were still going on in 1988 when Douglas President Jim Worsham conceded that "it is very difficult for competitors to collaborate."

The talks with Airbus were abandoned, but by 1990 the cost of developing the proposed re-winged MD-12X trijet stretch had mushroomed to $3 billion with the realization that the wing would have to be much larger than previously thought. In all, it would have an area of 4,870 square feet—29 percent larger than the MD-11—with about 753 square feet more area than the A330/A340 wing. It would have had a

184-foot wingspan, compared with 211 feet for the 747-400.

But the worst was yet to come. Estimated costs had climbed to $4.5 billion by mid-1991, forcing McDonnell Douglas into a radical rethink. Instead of digging into its own dwindling coffers for development dollars, why not invite partners to share in the development? In return for taking this risk, the partners would be entitled to part of the profit. At the same time, MDC could benefit by sharing its own risk and by bringing in partners who could perform work at relatively low cost.

Gareth Chang, MDC president for Pacific and Asia, described in *Flight International* a paradigm shift in the company's strategy for regaining commercial market share. Production costs were to be driven down by putting work where labor costs were lower, while development capital would be sought from emerging nations preparing to invest in high-tech industries.

Casting its net wide to talk with companies in Japan, South Korea, Taiwan, and elsewhere, MDC hoped to offset more than 60 percent of its costs through the relatively novel concept of risk-sharing partnerships. To further encourage the move, which was pivotal to the launch of the MD-12X and with it the long-term survival of the company itself, MDC offered equity in Douglas in exchange for investment in the effort.

The first breakthrough seemed to come in November 1991 when MDC signed a memorandum of understanding covering equity investment by Taiwan Aerospace (TAC) and the possible formation of what was dubbed an "Asian Airbus." The negotiations dragged on, however, and MDC felt increasingly under pressure to give the MD-12 the go-ahead with or without TAC involvement. MDC still needed the cash, however, and Chang acknowledged that without Taiwanese involvement it would be "much tougher for us to keep our position and become competitive."

It was against this troubled background that the revised MD-12 plan was hatched. In overall appearance, the new design was similar in length to the MD-11 but, due to its twin-deck layout, would be capable of seating up to 450 in a three-class layout. Describing the MD-12 as "bold and visionary," Douglas President Robert Hood claimed that the big jet had "leapfrogged our competition and is, in short, an aircraft for the twenty-first century." Hood also believed the MD-12 would capture a fair share of the 2,500 aircraft worth $300 billion that MDC had forecast would be required in the long-range market over the next 20 years.

From the start it was clear that the MDC design had more in common with the new double-deckers Airbus had shown at the previous year's Paris Air Show than with anything Boeing had shown until then. The driving force behind the design, according to MD-12 Vice President Walt Orlowski, was the goal of beating the seat–mile costs of the 747-400

McDonnell Douglas had done so well with its stretched DC-8 and DC-9 derivatives that an extension of its DC-10 was considered a logical approach to the emerging 7,000-nautical mile, 300-passenger aircraft market. By the mid-1980s, McDonnell Douglas (MDC) predicted demand would be for as many as 1,400 aircraft by 1998. Although the project was launched as the MD-11 as early as December 1986, McDonnell Douglas failed to capitalize on its lead over the competing A340 and 777 programs that were subsequently given the go-ahead by Airbus and Boeing, respectively. The MD-11 did, however, sustain MDC well into the 1990s and provide the basis for several subsequent stretch attempts to compete in the "jumbo" market.
Mark Wagner

The baseline McDonnell Douglas Corporation (MDC) MD-12 would have measured 208 feet in length, with an identical span (213 feet) to the 747-400. Seating up to 511 in a high-capacity layout, the aircraft was a world away from traditional MDC designs with its double-deck, four-engined layout. The design also featured a three-axis fly-by-wire flight control system with wing load alleviation, extensive use of composites in the empennage, new four-post landing gear, and an unusual three-aisle main deck. The wing design included Douglas Aircraft's latest divergent trailing edge (DTE) feature, a patented design that Boeing later offered as the "trailing-edge wedge" on its proposed 747-400X and 747 Advanced. DTE helped wing performance by increasing the curvature near the trailing edge, thereby increasing the amount of aft camber and improving transonic lift distribution. *Author's Collection*

while at the same time meeting the payload/range goals its target airline group had established.

The fact was that Douglas could not meet these goals with a stretched MD-11. "Optimizing the fuselage cross section and length did nothing to help," Orlowski said. "We went from 10 abreast to 11 and 12, but the return was really poor, and it looked like we'd need 20 before we got what we really wanted. We needed an aircraft with the same weight as before but with more seats."

The new wing supporting the big double-decker was a key part of the design, which was meant for stretching from the start. The wing was designed with a divergent trailing-edge drag-reduction feature that Douglas had patented. It produced an effect similar to the variable-camber concept Airbus had studied for the A340, and gave the MD-12 wing both significant inverse, or aft, camber and a blunt trailing edge almost 1.5 inches deep. The divergent trailing edge was optimized for a Mach 0.85 cruise and promised a 3 to 4 percent improvement in overall aerodynamic efficiency.

Another reason for changing to four engines was the availability of appropriately rated new-technology turbofans. "We needed 240,000 pounds of thrust, which either means four engines of about 60,000 pounds each or three of 80,000 pounds. Our only choice for the trijet was a bigger engine (the General Electric GE90 was then in early development for the Boeing 777) and a de-rate, but this had big weight penalties," said Orlowski.

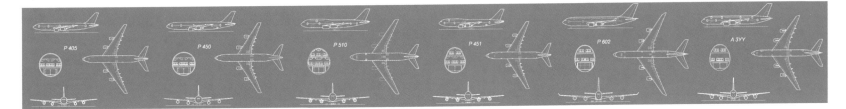

The early strands of A380 DNA are visible in these pre-A3XX UHCA concepts that trace the design activity among the Airbus partners in the 1991–1992 timeframe as they sought to define the best way forward. Note the single-deck P405 and P450 concepts, and the intriguing 747 look-alike P510 and P451 designs, the former sporting a five-post main undercarriage configuration. The best features of these designs, plus P602 (recognizable as DASA's A2000, see photo on page 22) were molded into the 3E P500 concept group in mid-1993. From here sprang the A3XX and its predecessor, briefly dubbed the A3YY. *Airbus*

It could be argued that the MD-12 was the first of the really viable new UHCA designs, but it was almost certainly the least likely to see the light of day, which proved to be the case. Douglas Aircraft, increasingly the victim of bad timing, unveiled the double-deck MD-12 in the midst of one of the worst recessions the airlines had yet seen. Orders for the already launched models were hard to come by, let alone those for a yet-to-be-launched multibillion-dollar gamble like the MD-12. In the first half of 1992, for example, Douglas took only four new firm orders for the MD-80/90 and no new business at all for the MD-11. The warnings were all there in 1991, when only 37 new orders had been booked for the whole year, compared with 188 in 1990. The year had been so bad, in fact, that Douglas had more cancellations than new firm orders placed or options exercised, with the backlog dropping by 25 percent during 1991 to just $17.9 billion.

Worse still, by entangling the MD-12 project with the complex attempts to sell up to 40 percent of Douglas to Taiwan Aerospace, MDC had sent the completely wrong message to the airlines, even those historically loyal to the company, such as American and Delta. Robert Crandall, the chairman of American Airlines, provided a classic example. Speaking to *Aviation Week & Space Technology*, he said, "The aircraft was okay. The problem was the financial condition of McDonnell Douglas. It is not in any shape to start a new aircraft program." While everyone suffered, Douglas was hurting the most, and the airlines knew it. In the same six months of a virtual drought in orders, Airbus had booked 77 while Boeing had notched up 113.

Crandall's words echoed throughout the industry as Douglas vainly sought to sign up customers for the MD-12 through the dry months of early 1992, as well

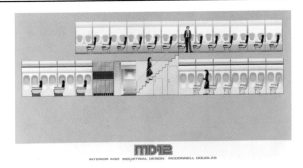

MD-12
INTERIOR AND INDUSTRIAL DESIGN MCDONNELL DOUGLAS

as coerce the Taiwanese into signing up on the deal. By June 1992, Douglas conceded that the orders were just not coming in and slipped the planned launch into 1993, claiming that the failure to seal the deal with Taiwan Aerospace had not affected the situation.

Increasingly desperate attempts to prop up the MD-12 continued as 1992 wore on. The fall issue of MDC's *Spirit* magazine that year, for example, proudly announced that the forthcoming super-sized airliner "will be the biggest—and the best—jetliner ever built." The article continued on a hopeful note, predicting that the MD-12 "could be the revenue earner that puts McDonnell Douglas on top in the commercial aircraft industry." It also said that the "introduction of the MD-12 gives MDC a head start over its competitors. Boeing is studying the concept of a 750-passenger wide-body, and an 800-passenger superjumbo is said to be under development at Airbus. But no such aircraft have yet been offered to customers."

What MDC failed to realize most was that, even as that particular edition of *Spirit* was landing on employees' desks, the MD-12 dream—and the Taiwan deal—were already dead. Research-and-development spending for the last quarter of 1992 was pared drastically back to about $11 million against the

A rather dated-looking artist's rendering from 1992 depicts the broad stairway close to door 1 on the proposed MD-12. The aircraft, had it been launched, was intended as the basis for a broad family of derivatives ranging from a 620-passenger, long-range (LR) stretch to a 430-seater MD-12 Twin. The MD-12LR would have been stretched more than 26 feet to a total length of 239 feet, enabling more than 700 passengers to be seated in a high-density layout. The tail would have also been increased from 74 feet high on the baseline to 82 feet on the -12LR. *Author's Collection*

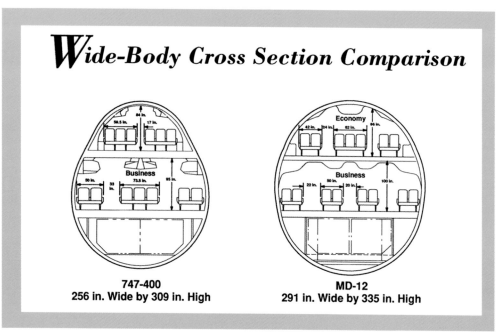

Wide-Body Cross Section Comparison

747-400
256 in. Wide by 309 in. High

MD-12
291 in. Wide by 335 in. High

Looking remarkably similar to the cross section of the later A3XX and A380, the MD-12 was sketched out with an overall width of 24 feet, 3 inches and a height of 27 feet, 11 inches. The early renditions of the A3XX, by comparison, showed an overall width of 22 feet, 10 inches and a height of 27 feet, 9 inches, later being revised upward on the A380 to 23 feet, 5 inches wide and 28 feet, 1 inch high. For all its promise, however, the MD-12 was doomed long before it even got to the proposal stage by the repeated failure of MDC to invest in its Douglas Aircraft product line and expand beyond its traditional twinjet and trijet derivative families. *Author's Collection*

$80 million spent over the first part of the year, and the MD-12 quietly died.

Airbus smelled blood, and despite MDC's subsequent attempts to reinvigorate the MD-11 with studies of a long-range variant, possible plans to develop new-generation twins, and the launch of the MD-95 100-seater, most airlines recognized that the end was not far off for McDonnell Douglas, the once proud aircraft manufacturer. In some ways, the dramatic and unexpected foray into the UHCA market had exactly the opposite effect that MDC had hoped for. The project briefly and brilliantly lit up the marketplace, but in the end it served only as a distress signal to tell the aviation industry that Douglas Aircraft was badly holed and sinking fast.

Airbus Narrows Focus

Unperturbed, and possibly encouraged, by the emerging Long Beach fiasco, Airbus spent the bulk of 1992 further defining its approach to the UHCA market and continuing its dialogue with 10 selected airlines. By October, the consortium revealed that it was focusing on a two-family design approach with a smaller version seating between 600 and 800, and a larger UHCA seating between 800 and 1,050.

Still loosely designated the A350 at this stage, the baseline UHCA was sketched out with a massive wing with an area of 8,020 square feet, compared with 3,900 square feet for the A330/A340. Span was set at 255 feet, and the mean aerodynamic chord or—the distance from the leading edge to the trailing edge measured parallel to the longitudinal axis—was a full 63 percent longer than on the A340 wing. The design also continued to be centered around two A340 fuselages married laterally to form a flattened ovoid cross section. Overall, the UHCA was to be about 260 feet long with a 51-foot-tall tail.

The smaller 600-seater had a planned payload of about 163,000 pounds, of which 30 percent was to be made up of belly freight. In a single-class high-density 800-seat layout of the type the Japanese airlines used on the domestic 747SR variants, the aircraft would have a payload of about 167,400 pounds but no capacity for freight. The larger family versions were similarly configured, with payload limits of up to 407,490 pounds and seating for as many as 1,050 in a single-class layout.

All the other weird and not-so-weird configurations were still in the melting pot of possible options at this stage, including the cloverleaf cross section that combined the fuselage of the A340 with that of an A320 on top, or a larger version with a new cross section on the main deck and an A340 scabbed on top. Maximum spans in the study ranged up to 275 feet, while the longest fuselages were up to 265 feet.

Supporting studies were underway to help answer all the other questions about developing the world's biggest airliner. Questions about simply how to deal with the unusual levels of mass and stiffness distribution within such a huge flexible structure; how to spread the weight of a 1-million-plus-pound aircraft on the wheels; how to steer the massive aircraft around existing airports and their limited taxiways; how to handle the flying controls; the noise it might create; and how to evacuate all the passengers in an emergency.

Meanwhile, Boeing's future large airplane studies, now being led by Chief Project Engineer John Roundhill, showed an all-new design that bore an even closer resemblance to the MD-12 than the first double-deck shapes revealed the year before. But Roundhill said the designs were "a lot different in detail. In general terms, one of the designs is short and fat. A circular cross section is our baseline, but there are variations."

The new design could seat up to 750 and was based on three different cross-sectional arcs in a triple-bubble configuration for added strength at reduced weight. The design also avoided the bulk of the structural problems Boeing encountered with the upper-deck fairing of the 747's section 41 nose section, while allowing the incorporation of an extremely wide main deck. For most configurations, this was 12 abreast, with 14 abreast studied for short-range domestic Japanese routes.

The new wing was designed to provide a 6 percent improvement in cruise efficiency over the 747-400, with about another 3 percent from the use of state-of-the-art engines. The use of hybrid laminar-flow techniques for drag reduction was also thrown into the pot as a way of achieving a Mach 0.865 cruise speed with low drag.

Like Airbus, the Boeing study included aspects of the infrastructure, including runways and ground handling. After reviewing 70 runways at the most likely key destinations around the world, the study estimated that 17 would require strengthening with an extra 3 to 6 inches of asphalt. Intriguingly, the study also recommended the use of closed-circuit TV cameras mounted in the empennage and belly to help prevent the crew from taxiing over the edges of runways and taxiways.

The study group had also split into two parts—one was focused on the 747X derivatives and the other was focused on the all-new design. No timetable was being publicly discussed, but Boeing Executive Vice President Phil Condit suggested that 1994 to 1995 would be prime time for launch. "Our thinking has to be five years out, in terms of delivering at the end of the century," he said. Not to be put off by the dire state of the industry that year—the conditions that were then condemning the MD-12 to death by a thousand cuts—Condit said: "If you look at our history, we always start making new aircraft in the middle of a recession and we always start delivering them in the middle of a recovery."

What Condit (or anyone else at the time) could not reveal was the fact that secret transatlantic talks had started over the future of the UHCA. The revelation would equally shock and confound the industry for several years to come, and the ultimate outcome of these talks would forever alter the destiny of both Airbus and Boeing.

Boeing's new large airplane (NLA) appeared in many guises to fulfill the emerging UHCA requirement. Most of the non-747–derived studies, such as this rendition, were based around an ll-new wing with 777 aerodynamic heritage, as well as 777-derivative engines. This behemoth could seat up to 750 passengers and had a "triple-bubble" fuselage cross section to incorporate an extra-wide main deck. *Boeing*

Daunted by the estimated $10 billion plus development costs of the next-generation superjumbo added to what it forecast would be a limited market, Boeing believed the only viable way forwa transport (VLCT) partnership. It predicted that in terms of expense and complexity, the superjumbo project would be on the same scale as a second-generation supersonic transport replacemen multinational experience of Concorde helped pave the way for the creation of Airbus. A British Airways Concorde, afterburners ignited, thunders off runway 27 right at London Heathrow to chas

Mark Wagner

3

Defining a Dream

Nineteen ninety-three was a mere five days old when Boeing and Deutsche Aerospace, a member of the Airbus consortium, dropped a bombshell on the aviation industry. To everyone's amazement, Boeing's UHCA project manager John Hayhurst and DASA chairman Jürgen Schrempp announced on January 5 that the two were joining forces on a UHCA or very large commercial transport (VLCT) feasibility study. Acting on contacts first made at the Farnborough Air Show the previous September, Schrempp and DASA aircraft group leader Hartmut Mehdorn had followed up with a visit to Boeing in late 1992. But the announcement posed far more questions than answers, the biggest question being whether or not Airbus itself was involved in the feasibility study.

As far as Airbus chairman Jean Pierson was concerned, the European consortium had already played a direct role. Speaking at the annual Airbus results conference in Paris early that January, Pierson declared that initial discussions had taken place at Farnborough between himself, Schrempp, and Hayhurst, and that at the end of the month the Airbus board was due to review a discussion document that the meeting had sparked.

However, the journalists at the meeting had also listened to the Boeing/DASA press briefing only a few days before and asked why Hayhurst had made no reference to Airbus. Pierson replied that, "either he does not remember me, which is impolite, or he has a short memory, which disqualifies him from being a project manager, or he's having second thoughts. I think it's more likely he's having second thoughts."

In making such a statement, Pierson indirectly admitted that Airbus had not been invited to participate in the VLCT study, even though one and possibly more of its mem-

German aviation engineer Jürgen Thomas is frequently referred to as the "father" of the A380. He was European project director of the VLCT study with Boeing and immediately afterward took the helm of the A3XX program by running the Airbus large aircraft division when it was formed in 1996. With the appointment of Charles Champion as head of the newly launched A380 program, Thomas took on a new role as special advisor to chief executive Noel Forgeard. *Airbus*

bers had. Pierson was adamant, however, that the move did not threaten to undermine Airbus or the consortium's continuing aircraft studies or those being conducted with the consortium's members. "There has been no betrayal by an Airbus member. This is not the end of the Airbus system," Pierson strongly reiterated.

The Boeing line was equally adamant. "We are open to working with member companies of Airbus, rather than Airbus itself. We think we will always compete with Airbus head to head. We will be just as vigorous in our competition as we expect them to be," a representative of the U.S. company said. Boeing also strongly denied that the move was aimed at anything other than studying the UHCA and vehemently denied that it was using subterfuge aimed at destabilizing Airbus or at driving a wedge between the partners in the consortium.

Boeing could not deny, however, that the link with DASA was extraordinary. So why was it established in the first place? The primary reason was the massive $10 billion, plus development costs, that Boeing estimated would be needed to see the new jumbo through development. Should it go ahead, the U.S. firm expected the project to be on the same scale as a second-generation Concorde replacement effort. In other words, something it considered to be well beyond the means of either Airbus or Boeing and demanding a broad international collaboration.

Second, there was the issue of market size. After its initial rush of enthusiasm, and the painful post–Gulf War period for the airlines, Boeing's view of the true size of the superjumbo market was changed. Its analysis predicted near- to mid-term demand from only a handful of international customers, nowhere near the market size that would be required to support competing designs.

Then there were other, less direct reasons related to the ever-changing tactical and strategic struggle for market share. For Boeing, faced with the task of getting the 777 through certification and into service, the talks with DASA would be extremely beneficial. First, it would give it a clearer and broader view of the true state of the market as well as the market's technical requirements. Second, it would almost certainly delay rather than speed up the entry into service of a 747 competitor. Boeing was clearly not in a position to make an early commitment to develop a new superjumbo, but by engaging DASA in this new dialogue, it would effectively slow Airbus' progress toward firming up a competitive program of its own.

With a supreme touch of irony, Boeing pointed out that the study couldn't really involve Airbus, even

if Boeing wanted it to. Boeing Corporate Vice President of Planning and International Development Larry Clarkson was keen to point out that as a GIE (Groupe d'Interet Economique) Airbus did not control the financial or physical assets of its member companies. The U.S. manufacturer, therefore, had no choice but to deal with these "real" companies instead. DASA would be first, but there would soon be more.

"We have left open the possibility of bringing in others to the study. These include our Japanese friends, Kawasaki, Mitsubishi, and Fuji, as well as Aerospatiale, British Aerospace, McDonnell Douglas, and the Russians. It's a pretty wide-open ball game," said Boeing, which explained: "The reason we're talking to DASA is that it is like Boeing: very diversified. Airbus is only one segment of their business. We can see ourselves doing business with them."

It was true. As a GIE, Airbus represented a group of independent companies with a joint family of products rather than a single company. The structure of the GIE, a uniquely French business concept, had been the perfect platform on which to float Airbus into the market. It allowed the companies to work closely together toward a common goal with a set of joint products, without having to operate under the tight legal and financial ties of a strict partnership.

Suddenly, and unexpectedly, the Boeing maneuver appeared to have left Airbus vulnerable and exposed. All the consortium's member companies remained free to work individually on aircraft outside the 100- to 350-seat range already covered by the existing Airbus product line, and there was nothing Airbus could do to prevent it. In the long run, however, Boeing's extremely clever move would prove to be a double-edged sword. By delaying the ultimate superjumbo development, Boeing unwittingly gave Airbus more time to make important design changes to accommodate new noise legislation. The initiative would also help accelerate Airbus toward a radical restructuring into a single entity that enabled it to launch a superjumbo and carry it forward into the twenty-first century.

Boeing, DASA, and the other main Airbus partners, Aerospatiale, British Aerospace, and CASA, signed a memorandum of understanding on January 22, 1993, that covered the start of the first phase of the VLCT study. Part of the agreement included the creation of "Chinese walls" within each organization to prevent the crossover of sensitive information between the various Airbus and Boeing large-aircraft project camps. John Hayhurst admitted at the time that the arrangement was "like walking a tightrope," but added that no formal timetable or structure for the study had been finalized. "We haven't resolved what details will be looked at specifically. The intent is to focus on things like, is this the right size? And so on. We want to reach a general understanding rather than get into specifics."

Hayhurst openly admitted that all parties would be forced, to some extent, to share their newly refined knowledge of large aircraft from their respective UHCA studies. "None of us is going in as complete neophytes," he commented. If the study was viewed as positive by the end of 1993, the plan was to look at details of joint manufacturing, but "for the moment it's going to take time to figure out how to work together," added Hayhurst.

While the new transatlantic VLCT team got down to work, Airbus and Boeing continued to plough their own furrows. Within days of Boeing's surprise VLCT gambit, Airbus made an informal offer to the Japanese aerospace industry for an "equal, risk-sharing partnership" of up to 30 percent of the UHCA. Airbus was increasingly anxious to outflank Boeing in Japan, where the U.S. manufacturer enjoyed a very close relationship with the aerospace industry and airlines. Loyal 747 users such as Japan Air Lines (JAL) and All Nippon Airways (ANA) were prime targets for the future UHCA, and increasing the Japanese industrial

work share was seen as crucial to winning the hearts of the airlines. Although Airbus had been sowing the seeds of a Japanese campaign for over a year, the VLCT maneuver injected fresh urgency into its efforts.

In late January 1993, Pierson presided over a series of meetings with the three main Japanese aerospace companies: Fuji, Kawasaki, and Mitsubishi Heavy Industries. "They would be offered a decision-making partnership in the UHCA program and be treated as equal partners throughout," said Airbus. Taking a swipe at Boeing, which had contracted large structural elements of several civil programs such as the 767 to the big three Japanese manufacturers, Airbus added: "We will not simply present them with a design which they will then be expected to build."

Airbus had also refined its market predictions, which showed a need for up to 727 UHCAs between 2001 and 2011. "Our forecasts indicate that 25 percent of the seats in as-yet-unordered aircraft in the next 20 years will be in UHCA-type aircraft. That's too important to leave in the hands of a Boeing monopoly," Airbus said. The studies also revealed that the average requirement was for an aircraft with 759 mixed-class seats. And perhaps not surprisingly, in a region where the 747 was jokingly referred to as a regional jet, the studies identified the Asia-Pacific

Airbus was not officially invited by Boeing into the 1993 VLCT study because, according to the U.S. company, it was not a "real" manufacturer. Airbus had, indeed, been formed under the auspices of a unique French business concept called a "GIE," which allowed it to represent a joint family of products made by a group of independent companies. The first of these products, the pioneering A300B, is pictured on its first flight in October 1972. *Airbus*

region as the key market, forecasting that 11 of the airlines in the region would need more than 30 UHCAs each, which together would account for 66 percent of the total demand for the aircraft.

Five of those same airlines were also working at the same time with Boeing, which spent much of 1993 attempting to define a new large airplane (NLA), or 747X. ANA, Cathay Pacific, JAL, Singapore Airlines (SIA), and Qantas Airways were involved, as were Air France, British Airways, and Lufthansa. It was a sign of the times that United Airlines was the sole U.S. representative.

The plan was to whittle down five favorite concepts to two versions by July 1993, and a single configuration by the end of the year. The studies, none of which were related to the parallel VLCT effort, gave birth to a variety of shapes and sizes, with seating between 550 and 630 passengers, and stretch capacity up to 750.

Only one of the five finalists was a 747 derivative, a massive 282 feet in length, allowing it to seat up to 550 in three classes. Although it was by far the longest aircraft, it was also the smallest in capacity. Two of the other finalists were double-deckers, one

was a model that looked like a 747 with an all-new cross section, and the fourth was a 244-foot-long single-deck monster.

Despite adopting as its baseline a double-deck design similar to those being studied by the VLCT and Airbus UHCA teams, Boeing had an inherent resistance to the concept. This went all the way back to the influence of veteran designer Joe Sutter, the acknowledged father of the 747. Although the 747 would be the only double-deck commercial jetliner in production for 35 years, the emergence of its distinctive upper-deck hump was originally driven not by passenger requirements, but by the needs of a freighter. The 747 design team always believed that most of the fleet would eventually be converted to freighters or made as freighters from the start. In the run up to launch in 1966, the 747 was therefore given a hinged nose section that allowed for straight-through loading but meant that the cockpit had to be moved up and out of the way. This created a de facto double deck, and passengers were only later accommodated in the upper deck, virtually as an afterthought.

Boeing had considered lots of full-up double-decker concepts in 1965 for launch customer Pan

American, but to Joe Sutter the designs produced "a clumsy airplane." Sutter's design team hit problem after problem when trying to fit everything into what he described as a "short, stubby airplane. The servicing of the aircraft, the door arrangement, the emergency evacuation situation, and the loading of cargo and baggage all became problems," he said in a 1997 interview.

There was, however, one early fan of double-deckers. This was none other than Charles Lindbergh, the famous aviator who had been the first to make a solo crossing of the Atlantic in 1927. In a letter to Pan American, to which he was a high-profile advisor, Lindbergh expressed his belief that a twin-deck design made the most efficient use of floor space.

Fast forward to 1993, and Boeing was once again looking at double-deckers. This time, instead of the six- and eight-abreast twin-deck designs of the 1960s, the new baseline was designed to take up to 624 passengers in three classes, with 18 abreast in economy! The aircraft was about 18 feet longer than a 747 and weighed in at about 1.4 million pounds. Other designs included an alternate double-deck seating for 584 and a huge single-deck design based on a 777-style fuselage.

Enter the A3XX

While Boeing's new concepts were grabbing the headlines at the 1993 Paris Air Show that June, Airbus was quietly approaching a critical juncture in its history. It was determined not to lose the initiative to Boeing and, spurred on by the challenge the VLCT conundrum posed, moved quickly to consolidate the results of the UHCA studies it had originally commissioned from the three main consortium members: Aerospatiale, British Aerospace, and DASA.

All three had come up with very similar double-deck designs that included Aerospatiale's ASX 500/600, which, as its designation suggests, was aimed at satisfying both the 500- and 600-plus-seat markets. BAe came up with a concept dubbed the AC14, while DASA's P502/P602 had by now become as familiar a shape—in model form—as the A2000 on every Airbus show display. Airbus took the best characteristics of each of the three designs and, during that hot June of 1993, blended them into an amorphous group called Family 1. The concept was called 3E P500 to reflect both its 3E technology-demonstrator designation and its baseline capacity of more than 500 seats. The family consisted of two major versions, the 3E P500-100 and a stretch -200 variant with higher capacity.

With hindsight, it's now possible to see Family 1 as the genetic grandfather of the A380 and the three main partner studies as the great-grandparents. Another great-grandparent was the rather strange horizontal double-bubble (HDB) design that Airbus had revealed earlier. Over the next four months, this later line would give birth to a more refined study with double decks seating seven abreast on each deck. More important, it gave Airbus a touchstone against which to judge the relative merits of Family 1.

But how was this to be done? It was obvious that Family 1 favored a conventional double-deck vertical design, while some within Airbus still believed that the unusual design of the HDB held merit. The only solution was to take it to the next stage and compete the concepts against one another, and it was to this end that in October 1993 Airbus announced the formation of the A3XX integration team. "For me, that was the big step forward, where we began seriously to compare the ovoid with the HDB," said Wissel, who would later become director of configuration integration for the A380.

By giving the study the A3XX designation, Airbus instantly raised the intensity of the UHCA/VLCT debate to a whole new level. The designation also provided a sharper focus for the design teams and, by bestowing it a pseudo-official Airbus identity, it spoke volumes to the market about the seriousness of Airbus' intentions. The 3E P500–derived Family 1 aircraft was renamed the A3XX-V600, with

Some idea of the typical everyday airport congestion found in Asia can be glimpsed in this dramatic image of a Garuda Indonesia A330-300 on very short finals to Hong Kong's old Kai Tak International shortly before operations there ceased and the new Chep Lap Kok International took over. The aircraft, one of six in the carrier's fleet, is operating the afternoon service from the Indonesian capital, Jakarta. *Mark Wagner*

35

an ovoid cross section carrying 10 abreast on the main deck and seven on the upper deck. The original Airbus UHCA HDB was renamed the A3XX-H600.

The integration team went straight to work and almost immediately cast aside the unusual but awkward A3XX-H600 in favor of the V600 alternative. The team decided that the vertical ovoid cross section would be lighter and therefore could use updated versions of existing A330-type engines. Speaking about six months after the decision for ditching the H600 the then-general manager of research and technology, Joachim Szodruch, admitted candidly: "The advantages of the horizontal layout, especially in terms of fuselage commonality with the current models, were not as great as we thought."

Wissel recalled: "We went right through all the design and operating criteria—airport compatibility,

weight, emergency evacuation, everything. In the end we chose the ovoid because it offered more flexibility. The HDB was limited to an extent in the length to which it could be stretched, and had these tie rods in the middle for load bearing that were a bit of a problem as far as the interior was concerned." Worse, the wind tunnel tests had not revealed any of the hoped-for lift contribution from the wide fuselage, so the HDB concept was dumped.

Parallel backup studies on the baseline 3E P500 concept drifted through the winter of 1993–1994 but would gradually fade away over the next four months as the A3XX firmed up around the -V600 vertical ovoid concept that would henceforth mark the fundamental configuration of the new aircraft.

Speaking in later years about the decision, A380 Senior Vice President for Engineering Robert

Lafontan said: "There is no better fuselage configuration than that of a wide-body on top of a wide-body. If you have a narrow-body mated to the top of a wide-body then it is too restrictive. There is no room for growth. If you have a wider [single-deck] body then the evacuation rules make it uneconomical. A wide-body on top of another wide-body is also capable of being a good freighter."

In January 1994, Airbus emerged with a single concept that would form the basis for its talks with airlines and that would eventually become the A380. The initial A3XX was divided into two main versions, the -100, provisionally seating about 500, and the -200 seating about 600. Airbus designers were determined to focus on keeping cost, complexity, and weight to a minimum from the outset, and as a result began the A3XX design with just three main gear legs in the tradition of the A340. But it soon became obvious that for system redundancy and pavement loading considerations, Airbus would have to follow the 747's lead and spread the weight over four main gears.

By March 1994, these changes were incorporated into a wider package of updates to the design that also included moving the entire wing slightly aft to achieve a better center of gravity, stretching both the -100 and -200 by two fuselage frames, and increasing the cabin volume by shifting the aft pressure bulkhead, or rear dome, farther back. The additional space created sufficient room for up to 530 seats in the -100 and 630 in the -200. "Making the cabin wider than the 747 was a big argument," recalled Wissel, "because laterally airlines can't do a lot with an extra 10 or 15 inches, but increasing the cross section gives them a lot more options when it comes to seat width."

The sudden acceleration of activity in the A3XX coincided with an extension of the VLCT study from the planned end date of January 1994 to April 1994. The partners had to decide on whether to extend the study phase or define a potential consortium, and they were facing increasing pressure from all sides.

Although DASA's Jürgen Thomas, the leader of the European partners, said that the VLCT was not "an undermining of their [Airbus] activities," the consortium was increasingly vocal in its objections to the study. Boeing, on the other hand, faced potential hurdles created by the U.S. government. John Hayhurst, now Boeing's vice president for large airplane development, said that some form of antitrust clearance would have to be obtained from the U.S. Department of Justice if a joint program were to be implemented.

Sure enough, as the A3XX concept gained momentum, cracks began to appear in the VLCT

team. Jürgen Thomas, then DASA's executive vice president of preliminary design and technology, conceded in January 1994 that, although it was clearly established Airbus policy to allow both the VLCT and A3XX studies to go ahead in parallel, there would be no possibility of both projects going ahead, because "there's just not enough room in the market."

Airbus itself added that it "would be difficult to see how we could cooperate with Boeing on a large aircraft and be at loggerheads with them on everything else. We do not believe they [the Airbus partners] would want to do something that would damage their interests in Airbus Industrie. There is no intention for Airbus to do one aircraft and the partners to do another." Thomas reinforced the view, adding that, "Airbus Industrie must stay in strong competition with Boeing." In what must be considered one of the understatements of the decade, he summed up the situation by saying that Airbus and Boeing cannot cooperate.

With the end of the extended VLCT phase looming, however, it was Airbus' turn to surprise the industry. At a meeting of the VLCT partners' chairmen in London on March 3, 1994, it was decided to extend the study into mid-1995 but, most puzzling of all, the "gang of five" announced that Airbus would be joining as an advisor.

Boeing said that, "the original agreement is still between Boeing and the four companies. But there are still some activities which they perform better as the joint [Airbus] entity." Behind the rhetoric, however, was an increasing atmosphere of uncertainty and, above all, suspicion between the U.S. and European

Boeing's aborted 1990s VLCT contrasted starkly with its earliest attempts in the 1960s to develop a double-deck 747 concept. These produced nothing more than a "clumsy airplane" according to the original design chief, Joe Sutter. The design suffered from inadequate baggage and lower deck cargo capacity, and effectively put off Boeing from looking seriously again at double-decker designs for many years. *Boeing*

Looking significantly different than today's A380-800, the early A3XX concept was pictured with a smaller area wing of reduced span and a far smaller belly fairing than the final design. The forward fuselage and nose shaping was also distinctly different, as was the vertical fin that, although the same overall height as the current design, was almost twice the chord. Note also the additional forward upper deck exit, which was later deleted from the -800 design, and the blunt tips of both the wings and horizontal stabilizers. *Airbus*

camps. Aerospatiale, in particular, made little secret of its misgivings, while senior Boeing figures within the study began questioning who was gaining the most out of the project.

Although the VLCT teams were separated by Chinese walls from their respective NLA and A3XX project teams, news about one another's projects frequently leaked through. Details of Boeing's stretched 747X plan, for example, told the Europeans that the U.S. company was studying an aircraft with a maximum takeoff weight of some 420 tons and a range of up to 7,700 nautical miles. The variant was based around an all-new wing using 777-style aerodynamics.

The news did not sit well with some. Speaking to *Flight International* in June 1994, Aerospatiale's director of aircraft programs, Claude Terrazoni, suggested that the move clearly indicated a hidden Boeing agenda. "If Boeing launches the 777B [referring to what would eventually become the 777-300ER rather than the -200ER], this will be in direct competition with the 747-400. Boeing will therefore be obliged, in order not to kill its 747 market, to push the

Jean Roeder's idea of trying to make the UHCA concept affordable by mating two A340 fuselages side-by-side was pivotal to the birth of the horizontal double-bubble (HDB) study and the gathering momentum of the A3XX. If the HDB had been chosen as the baseline design, the early stages of today's A380 assembly line could have looked something like this. Two forward fuselages await mating with the center fuselage and wing sections. As visible proof of the production standardization and modular approach Airbus adopted, these two identical sections were destined for very different outcomes. The aircraft in the foreground became a Cathay Pacific A330-300, while the fuselage behind it became an Air France A340-300. *Mark Wagner*

747 toward a bigger aircraft. It's what Boeing is actually doing now. We have proof. They're studying a new wing for the 747."

But Boeing argued that, like Airbus, it was within its rights to study legitimate options to the VLCT. In the meantime, it was all light and sweetness between the partners as the VLCT project moved onto phase two, with an agreed agenda covering a refined market forecast, first steps toward a possible joint business arrangement, and key technical issues. These included airport changes to cope with a VLCT, including wing span limitations on runways, taxiways, and aprons; weight on crossover bridges; fuel, cargo, and passenger volumes; noise levels; and emergency evacuation from double decks.

What was not widely known outside the closed sessions of the project was that the VLCT team had decided to shrink the aircraft slightly. Switching gears in a subtle way, phase two was to examine the arrangements of a European-inspired 500- to 550-seat design versus the Boeing-led 600-plus seater studied in phase one. The move, which would have seemed relatively unimportant to outsiders at the time had they known about it, was to have much more serious ramifications in the years to come.

British Airways was by now making the most encouraging noises to the manufacturers, who refined their market predictions to between 450 and 500 aircraft with more than 500 seats by 2010. Cathay Pacific's managing director, Rod Eddington, said his airline might be interested in a VLCT, but only a relatively short-range version compared with the mega-ranges being studied.

More ominously, American Airlines' influential chairman Robert Crandall said simply: "We just don't think that bigger airplanes are the way to go. Smaller aircraft with longer ranges are the way to go." These few words, spoken almost casually in March 1994, were to resonate with Boeing's top leadership and help nudge it toward a seismic shift in strategy that would soon doom the company's VLCT and NLA while giving Airbus a free hand in the superjumbo market of the twenty-first century.

By January 1995, planning was under way on where to take the VLCT study beyond mid-July, when phase two was due to end. If all sides agreed that the market was sufficiently large, the plan was to begin evaluations of a common configuration later that year. Thirty-eight individual teams ramped up their frequent-flyer accounts as they

While the VLCT study was underway, some influential potential customers such as American Airlines began leaning more toward the concept of smaller, longer-range aircraft rather than larger aircraft for trunk routes. American, which had been involved in the airline advisory group on the design of the Boeing 777, eventually opted for this approach in 1996 and took delivery of 45 -200ERs from 1999 to 2003. *Mark Wagner*

crisscrossed the Atlantic to meet at least once a month. Airbus attended all the European planning meetings and maintained a broader presence by having representatives sit on the study's steering committee. Lawyers were also on hand at every working group meeting, and everyone was briefed on antitrust law.

Specific targets included discussions about launch criteria, putting a joint venture together, financial viability, common product development standards, laying out of key milestones, program integration, and sorting out the value of work packages in the event of a go-ahead.

But there would be no go-ahead. While phase two was getting into its stride, Boeing's independent re-winged 747X study had meanwhile mutated into a two-family double-stretch pair dubbed the -500X and -600X. The new wing had a broader chord than the existing design, and just fitting it to the fuselage created a slight stretch that would create space for between 500 and 600 passengers. Based on the same

wing, Boeing believed it could also develop a larger stretch variant capable of seating as many as 800, if the market needed it.

But did it? Even as Boeing's NLA team reported encouraging figures from its 747-500X/600X studies, the strategic thinkers within the company continued to echo the thoughts of Crandall. The then-president of the Boeing Commercial Airplane Group, Ron Woodard, said in May 1995: "The challenge is: will the Pacific marketplace fragment? History has shown that the Atlantic fragmented when the twinjets appeared—nearly all of them 767s." Boeing at the time was busy developing longer-range variants of the 777 with exactly this fragmentation phenomenon in mind.

Then there was the risk. A stretched, re-winged 747 conservatively pegged at about $4 billion to develop seemed a lot less risky and costly than the European partnership and its estimated $10 to $12 billion price tag. "We are convinced a company the size of Boeing would be threatened, even if we were in a partnership,

All the while Boeing and Airbus were engaged in the VLCT, the U.S. company was simultaneously working on a more conventional but relatively ambitious pair of 747-400 derivatives: the -500X and -600X. The -500X incorporated a new wing, a slight fuselage stretch, and new engines to carry 460 passengers in three classes on ranges of more than 8,700 nautical miles. The -600X used the same wing and would have a fuselage almost 50 feet longer than the -400. Capable of ranges up to 7,700 nautical miles, it was configured to carry up to 550 passengers in three classes, or virtually the same capacity as the A380. *Mark Wagner*

if the marketplace wasn't there," said Woodard. "We remain convinced that there is only room for one aircraft the size of a VLCT, and we will pursue this development only if it makes economic sense." There was no doubting the determination of Airbus, however, and Woodard added prophetically: "Airbus is eager to go it alone and launch the A3XX."

The writing was on the wall for the VLCT and, in July 1995, the final meeting of the teams at a hotel in Long Island, New York, brought this strange chapter in the superjumbo story to a close. The Boeing team headed west, and the European teams returned across the Atlantic—from now on it was back to the bitter cut and thrust of competitive warfare between the commercial giants.

"The VLCT caused some confusion," recalled Wissel. "There were just some points where we could not go any further with the discussions. Cockpit philosophy was a big one, what with our side sticks and Boeing with their conventional joystick. It was a big barrier to cross-crew qualification, and the product had to be compatible with the other products for both parties. It was really impossible. You couldn't build a cockpit with a conventional stick on one side and a side stick on the other! In the end we were happy when it ended."

The gradual growth of the A3XX, seen best in the progressive increases in wing area, fuel capacity, takeoff weight, payload, and range soon overcame the thrust capability of the derivative A330 design. The wing was also originally expected to feature variable camber "shape shifting" and possibly even laminar-flow (boundary layer) control technology to improve the cruise efficiency of however, in favor of a simpler, lighter single-slotted flap design and a more advanced, aft-loaded aerodynamic wing cross section. *Mark Wagner*

4

Manifest Destiny?

Long before the European VLCT partners recognized that the joint effort with Boeing was doomed, they had already learned a vital lesson. There was simply no way a project of this scale could be managed under the existing Airbus GIE structural arrangement. Something would have to change.

But Airbus was in an unusual position. It had grown and prospered under the GIE structure, but as Airbus became larger and more successful, the limitations of the business structure were obviously beginning to hamper growth. It could not, for example, make the most of the economies of manufacturing enjoyed by Boeing and McDonnell Douglas and, as Jean Pierson observed, had effectively reached its "genetic limits."

Under the GIE, Airbus was effectively a coordination and sales operation, not a manufacturer—exactly the excuse Boeing used to justify not inviting it to participate in the VLCT. As much of the design and manufacturing of the Airbus aircraft was carried out by the partners, any savings that came out of improvements in cost or design were enjoyed by the partners and their subcontractors rather than by Airbus itself. As a result, the savings could not be passed on to the airlines.

Due to the same restrictions, Airbus had far less ability to negotiate price reductions with its suppliers and partners than did Boeing. The bottom line was that Airbus was unable to take a lead on price, and this too would have to change before any A3XX launch was possible. In addition, Airbus' ability to raise money for big projects or forge new relationships outside the traditional partnership was very limited. Worse still, although Airbus could not take advantage of manufacturing cost reductions realized by its partners, it was still vulnerable if any of them suffered financially.

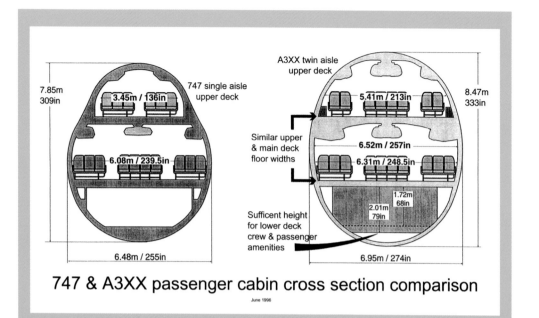

747 & A3XX passenger cabin cross section comparison

June 1996

Battle of the cross sections. While design engineers worked out the technical solutions, the Airbus marketers worked on ways to beat Boeing's 30-year dominance with the 747. The heart of the matter, they eventually figured, was cabin cross section and the ability to offer more space and comfort, regardless of deck or class of seating. With the basic ovoid sufficiently large to absorb containers below the main deck, the designers were free to explore interesting possibilities. Ultimately, they went further than the promises being offered here in 1995. The A380 ended up with a maximum main deck width of 21 feet, 7 inches, compared to the 747's 20 feet, 1 inch, while the upper deck not surprisingly was 46 percent wider with a width of 19 feet, 5 inches. *Airbus*

In view of this long-term losing proposition, the German and U.K. governments in particular had begun to put pressure on the partners to set up a more independent corporate structure. They believed that such a change would allow Airbus to take tighter control of costs as well as gain access to funds on its own account. Pierson listened, and in response a panel of "wise men" representing the Airbus partners was set up and tasked with reporting its findings on the question by mid-1996.

As if to emphasize the importance of the restructuring initiative, and thereby the foundations for the A3XX, the 1995 year-end sales figures came as a sobering reminder of Airbus' true market position. Once again the figures showed that Boeing had regained overall dominance in the market, which was showing signs of recovering from the dire days of the 1992 downturn. What was most striking, however, was the major impact of the 747 in combination with the 777. Heavyweight airlines such as SIA, KAL, and South African Airways (SAA) had all added 747s as well as the big Boeing twin.

In 1995, Boeing netted 39 new sales of 747s, worth (at least on paper) a staggering $6.5 billion, and dramatically highlighted the inability of Airbus to compete at the high-value end of the market. In a message to Airbus staff at the start of 1996, Jean Pierson said the consortium was intensifying design and development of the A3XX, adding that Boeing could not be left to dominate the market with the 747. Just four days later, Boeing once more raised the stakes

by announcing plans to begin a marketing campaign for its two major derivatives, the 747-500X and -600X, headed by former Boeing VLCT lead John Hayhurst.

With a mounting sense of urgency, Airbus sketched out plans for a large aircraft division that would bring together personnel from the partner companies and from Airbus itself. The combined team would be led by an A3XX program director—none other than Jürgen Thomas—and effectively marked the beginning of a process that would culminate with the total restructuring of Airbus itself and the launch of what would become the A380. Announcing the new division in March 1996, Airbus Strategic Planning Vice President Adam Brown said the organization would also "work closely with key potential customers to define the aircraft."

Other forces were also at work helping to push Airbus toward a restructuring that, in earlier forms, had often foundered on French objections. Although the chairman of Aerospatiale, Louis Gallois, remained "cautious" over moving too quickly on a radical re-jigging of Airbus, French transport minister Bernard Pons himself added to calls for action on the basis that the existing structure was making Airbus uncompetitive.

Just as plans were being announced to create the large aircraft division in early 1996, a leading credit rating agency, Moody's Investors Service, downgraded Airbus because of concerns over the effect of the possible restructuring. The concerns were as much about what the move away from GIE status might bring as they were about the uncertainty over what would follow. Moody's believed that Airbus could suffer because of weakened links with its partners and, without knowing much about the plans for the restructuring, could not recommend a higher debt rating.

Almost immediately after Moody's downgraded Airbus, BAe Chief Executive Dick Evans added his voice to the turmoil, saying that there was little prospect that the U.K. manufacturer would lend approval to the A3XX plan "unless there is a satisfactory restructuring running in parallel." To Evans it was clear that the fate of the A3XX and the long-term reorganization of Airbus were intimately entwined. Under the GIE structure, the four consortium companies took responsibility for funding on their own balance sheets, and BAe simply could not see any easy way to raise finance in its own right at interest rates in excess of 10 percent for an $8 billion project with a long-term payback like the A3XX. Under its launch plan, Airbus had told the partners that it expected to raise up to 30 percent of the money internally, 33 percent from refundable government loans and subsidies, and 40 percent from the risk-sharing partners and associates.

The restructuring panel meanwhile completed its report and presented its findings to the Airbus supervisory board, which on July 8, 1996, gave its approval to the proposal under which it would become a full-fledged company by the end of the decade. Although no firm timetable had yet been set, the partners agreed to begin immediate negotiations with the aim of drawing up a binding agreement by year end.

The partners finally signed a pledge on January 13, 1997, to reorganize the consortium amid pressure from the German government, which tied the transition to a single company and the launch of the A3XX to further research and development funding in aerospace. The move to restructure Airbus as a precondition for A3XX research funding was dubbed unrealistic by the German Aerospace Industries Association (BDLI), whose president, Manfred Bischoff, said: "To avoid unfair competition, we need a deliberate innovation policy for aviation in the future."

But Airbus and its partners faced a massive task in transforming from a consortium into a company. The January agreement drew up a blueprint that called for the full range of design and development, production, procurement, and customer service tasks to be transferred from the partners to the new Airbus. Having a plan was one thing; converting it into reality was quite another.

Arguments soon erupted between Aerospatiale and DASA over the valuation of the various sites contributing to Airbus, while the picture was further complicated by ongoing merger talks between the French manufacturer and Dassault Aviation. Other hurdles arose over a wide range of issues involving everything from taxation to employment rules, while deep-seated political and even cultural concerns were never far below the surface. The result would be a torturous restructuring process that would take far longer than anyone would have guessed.

Refining the A3XX

While the complex issues of recreating Airbus went on around them, the newly established Airbus large aircraft division team pressed on with refining the embryonic A3XX, which had already changed dramatically over the previous year.

In the intervening months since the start of the VLCT phase two work in 1994, the Airbus designers made more fundamental changes to the all-important

cross section. These included increasing the overall width to allow 10-abreast seating on the main deck, while adding extra width to the upper radius of the ovoid to provide space for up to eight across on the top deck. The move represented a return to the main-deck size recommended by the original vertical DB studies of the A3XX-V600 in late 1993 but added considerably to the capacity of the upper deck.

By this stage, Airbus had studied more than 40 cross sections and was totally focused on meeting the demands of as many airlines as it could. "If you get it wrong, it is wrong forever," said Thomas, who described the interior as the "biggest passenger cabin in history." The latest widening had come in response to airline feedback and allowed Airbus to configure the main deck with four seats in the middle and three on each side. This avoided what Airbus famously referred to as the "prisoner" middle seats in the five-abreast arrangements found on U.S. wide-bodies.

Airbus briefed 13 airlines on the progress of the superjumbo at a meeting held that summer in the medieval city of Carcassonne, in the south of France. Boeing was briefing the same airlines about the 520-seat

747-600X, which the U.S. manufacturer was touting with a 2000 delivery target date—three years ahead of the A3XX—so it was therefore vital for Airbus to drive home the advantages it claimed for an all-new design. Most important, said Thomas, was an estimated 17 percent lower seat–mile operating cost with the initial A3XX-100, and up to a 23 percent lower cost with the -200.

With the end of the VLCT the previous summer, Airbus also felt free to compare its baseline (then dubbed A3XX Status 7) with the results of the transatlantic study in October 1995. The results of this comparison, added to the earlier decisions to up the cross section and increase the overall size of the fuselage, led to more big changes in the next iteration, Status 8, which was reviewed in May 1996.

The airlines at the Carcassonne meeting heard new details about these latest changes, which included the vital decision to use all-new engines and build in more room for range and derivative growth by increasing the wing area. The gradual growth of the A3XX, and particularly the -200, meant that Airbus had to abandon its plan to use A330 engines. The plane's 72,000- to 80,000-pound thrust requirement actually overlapped the A330 engines at its lower end, but they ran out of steam at the higher end.

Explaining the dilemma, Thomas said: "The engines are adequate for the initial versions of the A3XX, but not for the growth variant, whereas the Boeing 777 engines would need to be de-rated, and would be too big, heavy, and costly." Luckily for Airbus, it knew that options would be available from Rolls-Royce, which was discussing a new Trent 800 development called the Trent 900, and from the General Electric/Pratt & Whitney Engine Alliance, which had already embarked on the similarly sized GP7000 engine for the 747X derivatives (see Chapter 10).

The larger wing, which was increased from 7,804 square feet to 8,396 square feet, provided capacity for up to 639,000 pounds of fuel for both models. With an aspect ratio of 8, the wing was designed to give the aircraft a range of 7,450 nautical miles and was approximately 40 percent larger than the 747-400's wing. At this stage the wing did not have winglets, though Airbus said that folding wingtips were still being considered as a serious option.

The wing was also expected to feature the variable camber innovation that had been considered, but not selected, for the A340. This was intended to reshape the aerofoil section to optimize it for particular stages of flight by adjusting the position of the leading- and trailing-edge slats and flaps. The technology was

considered sufficiently mature for introduction on the A3XX, but, as shall be seen, it would not be a feature of the final aircraft. Laminar-flow control, which offered potential performance benefits by closely controlling the boundary layer over the wing surface, was also considered but not implemented.

Since Airbus pioneered the use of large-scale composites, it was no surprise to the airlines attending Carcassonne that even the wing design incorporated carbon-fiber composites in the primary structure outboard of the engines, as well as in the fin and horizontal tailplane. "The big challenge will be the dimensions of these structures, considering that the horizontal tailplane alone will be of a similar size to the entire A310 wing," said Thomas.

Other key features highlighted at the meeting included the not-unexpected decision to adopt a cockpit common with the A320/A330/A340 to give operators the benefit of cross-crew qualification among all modern Airbus types. For operators concerned about the ability of the design to meet the 90-second evacuation rule from one side of the aircraft, the -200 form of which could seat a staggering 966 passengers in a single-class layout, Airbus also reassured them with details of new solutions from slide and life raft manufacturers. The studies covered several accident scenarios, including nose wheel collapses that left aft-seated passengers some 50 feet above ground level.

The preliminary design freeze was set for the third quarter of 1997, with the final design freeze set for the following year. At this stage, Airbus still targeted full go-ahead in the third quarter of 1999 and initial deliveries in 2003. Some of the airlines at Carcassonne, faced with a growing dilemma of whether to opt for the earlier option of the new 747 or wait for the all-new A3XX, had asked Airbus if it could speed up delivery. Airbus was reluctant to do this for several reasons. First, it did not want to be exposed to the sort of low production rates it had to face in the early days of the A300, and it wanted guarantees of 40 to 50 aircraft per year at launch. Second, it was eager to get it right the first time rather than put an immature product into the market. Airbus had suffered initial problems of this sort with the early A340 and was anxious to avoid a repeat.

Accelerating a Giant

But the pressure was intense, and some within Airbus saw this as a glorious opportunity to derail the Boeing plan, which was using the earlier in-service target as its major trump card. The decision to switch to a faster track was made, and news of the change of heart

emerged in mid-September 1996 when the engine makers were asked to prepare more detailed specifications, which indicated an overall program acceleration of about one year.

The switch, driven by airlines such as British Airways, SIA, United, JAL, and Thai Airways International, allowed them to see much more detailed proposals on specifics such as fuel burn, range, payload, and direct operating costs. In concert with these moves, Airbus also decided to undercut the expected $200 million-plus price tag of the new 747 derivatives by offering the A3XX at "no more than $198 million," according to Airbus Senior Vice President John Leahy.

Plans by now covered three possible family variants, including a base 555-seat (three-class) A3XX-100 with a slightly increased range of 7,500 nautical miles; the stretched 656-seat -200; and a longer range, higher gross weight derivative of the -100, the -100R, that would be capable of flying 8,520 nautical miles.

The Airbus move appeared to outflank Boeing, which, until relatively late in 1996, had appeared certain to launch the first stretch of the 747 since its launch some three decades earlier. Throughout the year, it had seemed only a matter of time before the two derivatives were to be unleashed on the market, with entry into service of the first variant—the 546-passenger, 7,500-nautical mile-range 747-600X—expected to be about December 2000. The smaller -500X, carrying 487 passengers over longer ranges up to 8,150 nautical miles, was likely to follow in six months.

Safety was a fundamental design driver from the start of the A3XX effort, with a major focus being on a comprehensive system of multi-role slide/life rafts. For the sake of safe and speedy evacuation, Airbus treated the A3XX as two totally independent passenger decks with the aim of keeping the maximum velocity at the "toe end" of the upper deck slides as no greater than those certificated on current single-deck aircraft. The most challenging design case was the main deck 3L and 3R overwing doors that required an inflatable device that could allow passengers to escape back over the trailing edge and away from the rear of the aircraft behind the upper deck slides. *Mark Wagner*

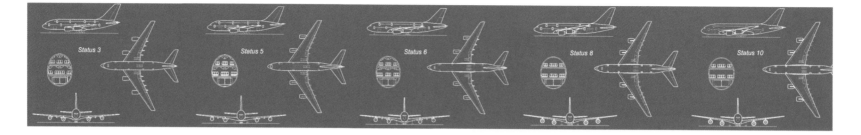

Status 3 Status 5 Status 6 Status 8 Status 10

So confident was Boeing that the new models would be launched and would succeed the -400, that new 747-400 contracts signed that year with British Airways and United included clauses allowing the operators to convert later delivery slots to -500Xs or -600Xs. The design was well advanced and revolved around a 777-style wing that reduced the 747's wing sweep from the almost 40-degree angle of the -400 to 36.5 degrees. The wing was also a massive 248.6 feet in span with an area of 7,540 square feet, but it was set to grow again to 255 feet in span and 8,100 square feet before its final completion.

Other aspects of the design included 777-style technology for the fly-by-wire flight control system, high-lift system, flight deck, power distribution, electrical and hydraulic systems, as well as the undercarriage. But the adoption of so much 777 technology was a calculated gamble for Boeing, which was torn between sticking to 747 systems and flight decks for commonality and moving to the newer technology for longer-term operating-cost benefits and faster development times.

John Hayhurst commented that the decision to use 777-style systems, for example, probably helped shorten the program schedule. "That's because the 777 systems are state of the art, and the team is mostly still here—to take that architecture and put it in the 747 is probably an easier task than updating the -400." In the short term, however, the wholesale adoption of radically newer technology had forced Boeing to virtually double its development cost estimates for the new derivatives to about $7 billion. To amortize this cost, Boeing also bumped up the price tag for the larger -600X version to a hefty $230 million in projected 2001 dollars compared to the then-list price of $165 million for the -400.

Despite the hurdles, Boeing held a final airline advisory group meeting at the end of August, on the eve of the 1996 Farnborough Air Show in the United Kingdom. The hopes were that Boeing would use the venue to announce the go-ahead of the project, stealing the limelight and maybe even the life out of the A3XX. Seven key carriers were in the frame to launch the 747X program, including British Airways, Cathay Pacific, Malaysia Airlines (MAS), SIA, and Thai.

Lufthansa, a loyal Boeing 747 operator and launch customer for the 737, was not among them. The airline's chief executive of operations, Klaus Nittinger, openly criticized the move away from commonality with the -400, saying that rather than improving the chances of launching the program the lack of commonality was damaging the program. He argued that costs had been driven up, which meant Boeing had been forced to increase seating capacity to keep seat–mile costs down. The extended fuselage of the -600X was, as a result, 16 feet, 5 inches longer than the 262-foot "box" it was generally agreed that future large aircraft would have to fit inside to be operationally feasible within the existing airport infrastructure. Nittinger added that even though the approach was aimed at favoring 777 operators, it would alienate more than it attracted. "Even those who were pushing for a bigger solution would still have bought a smaller aircraft with greater commonality with the -400."

Sure enough, things were all going to go sour for Boeing's planners, who were hoping to make the headlines at Farnborough. Part of the reason for this negative turn of events was that the airlines did not want to be railroaded into making decisions before they were ready. British Airways Chief Executive Robert Ayling said that it was "important not to go rushing into orders just because of meeting the deadline of some air show somewhere."

Without any firm consensus or even orders, other than outline "accepted proposals" for up to 15 aircraft from MAS and Thai, the planned December 1996 launch decision came and went. Over the company's traditional year-end break, senior officers faced the inevitable decision of whether or not to abandon the 747 growth plan. By now the -500X/600X project already employed more than 1,000 design and system engineers and was reputedly costing Boeing a staggering $3 million a day!

Boeing officially pulled the plug on the stretch plan at a board meeting in mid-January 1997, and announced it publicly on January 20. Boeing's product

At air shows around the world, models of the A3XX and 747-500X/600X vied for the attention of the attendees wandering the exhibit halls. All seemed pointed toward launch in the Boeing camp, so the sudden demise of the 747-500X/600X in early 1997 took much of the industry by surprise. Most surprised of all were those at the A3XX program who first heard about the decision on January 21 via one of the designated airline representatives working with Airbus on the definition of the superjumbo. Boeing cited insufficient market requirement as the main reason for the move, which came on the heels of the rollout of the first Next Generation 737 and the expensive takeover of McDonnell Douglas. The same rep then asked Airbus if they were about to can the A3XX for the same reason; the answer was an emphatic "No!" *Mark Wagner*

strategy and marketing vice president, Mike Bair, candidly admitted: "We just could not make a business case for it. The small size of the market meant the money we'd have to spend on it, with or without the affect of [route] fragmentation, just did not make sense."

Market reaction had been subdued for several reasons, although Bair said the aircraft itself was a "good one, with the 10 percent reduction in direct operating costs relative to those of the -400." What really killed it was a number of factors, not the least being the Airbus decision to accelerate the A3XX, thereby throwing a wrench in Boeing's calculated works.

Wall Street reacted enthusiastically, with Boeing stock moving up by more than $7, or about 6.9 percent, on the news. After all, mused analysts, not only

would the $7 billion be better spent on long-range developments of the 777, but the move would also prolong the life of the 747-400, which had just had a stellar year with 75 orders in 1996. Boeing, they argued, had bigger fish to fry after all. It was newly into the throes of taking over archrival McDonnell Douglas and had just bought big chunks of Rockwell as part of a concerted effort to grow its defense and space businesses. Besides, they said, there was always time later to develop better versions of the 747-400 when the market called for it. Who needs a superjumbo anyway? Let Airbus go ahead and build it!

Taking advantage of the fly-by-wire system to help control the stability of the aircraft artificially, Airbus was able to design a slightly smaller, and therefore structurally lighter, horizontal stabilizer. The elevators are all made from a lightweight monolithic CFRP design for additional weight saving—an essential consideration for a structure that measures almost exactly 100 feet in span! *Mark Wa*

5

Seeking Commitments

Boosted by Boeing's sudden decision to shelve the 747 derivatives, Airbus continued to refine the A3XX and work toward an initial design freeze that was still scheduled for the end of 1997.

Airbus prided itself on being innovative, and in its fight for market share against Boeing and McDonnell Douglas it had often used technology as a trump card in new designs such as the fly-by-wire A320. But now Airbus faced an embarrassment of riches as it surveyed the next-generation possibilities for the A3XX.

These included everything from avionics and in-flight entertainment to advanced design and assembly techniques. Anticipating the research and development (R&D) needs of the massive project, Airbus had created a formal initiative involving the four main partners in 1996, aimed at identifying where the main focus should be. Dubbed the 3E Plan (environment, economy, and energy), it was seen as a vital part of the battle to keep development costs under control.

By coordinating R&D efforts, Airbus hoped to eliminate duplication between study programs underway throughout the consortium and, at the same time, promote a cross-fertilization of ideas and solutions. Part of the 3E Plan was aimed at reducing the weight and maintenance cost of aircraft systems and included making less do more. Inspired by Honeywell's aircraft information management system (AIMS) used on the 777, Airbus hoped to utilize fewer avionics computers that would serve multiple roles.

Other projects included extending the use of aluminum electrical cable, designing servo controls with sufficient power to actuate the A3XX's massive horizontal tail surfaces, and harmonization of aluminum welding procedures. Further projects included studies into the use of titanium in the landing gear, carbon-composite primary structure in the outboard sections of the wing, and laminar-flow control around the engine nacelles.

Airbus also continued to tackle some fundamental configuration issues ranging from the location of the engines on the wing to the possible use of a forward fuselage-mounted foreplane. The latter option, which had appeared in April 1996 in the first artist's impressions of the A340-600, was tested as an option for aerodynamically off-loading the horizontal stabilizer. With concerns over drag and the size of the actuators, BAe Airbus conducted preliminary wind tunnel tests at its Bristol, Filton, site of a configuration with "canard wings" mounted on the upper fuselage crown area aft of the flight deck.

The concept was dropped from the A340-600 because of worries that the canard would interfere with the operation of jet bridges, and also because their effect was relatively minimal. Initial results from the A3XX were, on the other hand, more positive. But the idea of the large structures, which were approximately half the span of the horizontal tailplane, was soon dropped as being impractical. Like the -600

study, the benefits simply did not justify the additional complications.

The engine location change came as part of the Status 9b design update when both engines were moved outboard, the outermost being relocated to about 60 percent of the span. This change helped the designers reduce the structural weight of the wing by allowing them to take more advantage of the bending moment relief provided by the mass of the outboard engine. This essentially let the weight of the outboard (and to a lesser extent inboard) engine oppose the upward lifting force on the wing structure, thereby reducing the need for excessive structural stiffening.

At the same time, Airbus also opted for a revised frame pitch, which, aft of the more conventionally assembled nose section 11/12, upped the overall spacing between the frames running the length of the fuselage. Compared with all its other designs, which had 21-inch frame spacing, Airbus opted to make the frame spacing more proportional to the aircraft's size. The result, as seen in the final design, was a frame approximately every 25 inches. Airbus was, after all, planning the world's biggest airliner, and extra frame spacing would likely allow a wider range of interior options as well as less structural weight.

The Status 9b changes coincided with increasing concerns that development costs were rising like an inexorable tide and were already heading toward an estimated $9 to $10 billion. There were several factors, not the least being the growing R&D investment that would be needed to support technological developments to meet the cost-performance goals Airbus set. The development road map was becoming increasingly complex with potential new market opportunities falling out of Boeing's axing of the 747-500X.

In response to requests from Lufthansa and others, Airbus began in mid-1997 to study a reduced-capacity 480-seat aircraft that would have been a new member of the family joining the initial 7,500-nautical mile-range, 550-seat A3XX-100 and the longer range -100R version, along with the larger 656-seat A3XX-200. The new variant, soon to be dubbed the A3XX-50, was shortened by about 16 feet, and was to be offered with derated engines and lower takeoff weights.

From the start, Airbus had envisioned a full family of derivate models, including full freighter and multi-role cargo/passenger combis. The workload, therefore, included background studies on the freighter, dubbed the -100E, as well as the -100C

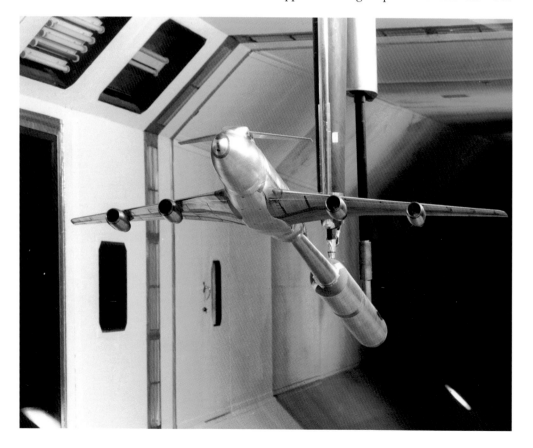

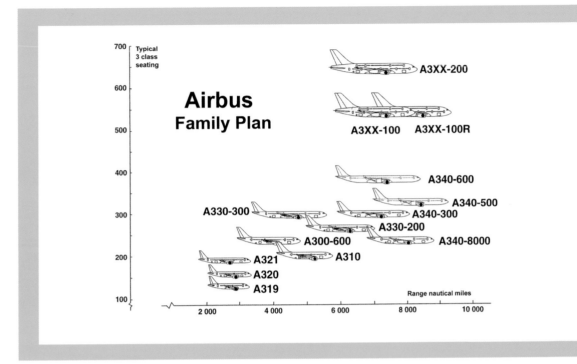

Airbus Family Plan

Typical 3 class seating

A3XX-200
A3XX-100 A3XX-100R
A340-600
A340-500
A330-300 A340-300
A330-200 A340-8000
A300-600 A310
A321
A320
A319

Range nautical miles

combi. Giant U.S. package freight company FedEx pushed along studies of the -100E and told Airbus that it needed capacity earlier than it expected.

To add to the workload, development of the new A340-500 and -600 derivatives was by then well underway, and the consortium's engineering resources were being stretched to the limit. On top of this, Airbus was coming to the glum realization that the performance figures from wind tunnel tests and other preliminary analyses were simply not good enough. Airbus knew that if it could not meet the cost savings target of 15 to 20 percent over the 747-400, it could not launch the A3XX.

The preliminary design freeze was accomplished on January 22, 1998, about a month later than planned but still pretty much on schedule, according to Philippe Jarry, vice president of market development at the large aircraft division. Jarry was speaking at the Singapore Air Show, where the deepening gloom of the Asia-Pacific economic crisis was taking center stage. It was also the first venue at which Airbus was able to explain why, only a few weeks before, Pierson had made the difficult decision to extend the entire development program by at least nine months, and possibly a full year.

Slowing a Giant

Officially the Asian economic crisis was not to blame. Airbus described it as "only a blip that will have

Titanium is used for the bulky main landing gear, which is integrated at Goodrich's site in Toulouse before final delivery to the assembly line. Engineers install a side-stay on a wing landing gear unit destined for one of the first Singapore Airlines aircraft. *Mark Wagner*

no effect on our long-term planning." Unofficially, however, Airbus was still looking for risk-sharing partners, particularly in Asia, and the financial meltdown of the region's Tiger economies had not only impacted long-term fleet expansion plans, but had dampened investment across all industries, including aerospace.

The real reason behind the move, however, was that the new design was not yet achieving the vital 15 to 20 percent cost reductions. Airbus knew that there was no way the new aircraft could be launched by the target date of late 1998. Even worse, Airbus had to acknowledge that a game plan to reach those cost savings had still not been resolved. In a statement, Airbus said: "We will launch only when we are satisfied that this aircraft meets cost specifications and provides the right level of return on investment for the airlines that will operate it."

Pierson's reign at Airbus was drawing to a close and, at his final official press conference before standing down at the end of March, he used the Asian show to spell out Airbus' determination not to rush into the A3XX. Areas still needed to be addressed, he said, including aerodynamics, cost-effectiveness, and aero-elasticity. The teams had been given another nine months to come up with the goods. And if they didn't, Pierson said that he would recommend a further delay.

While Pierson was enjoying a characteristic swan song in Singapore, engineers at the large aircraft division were working on Status 10a, the stage of formally incorporating the shorter-bodied A3XX-50 into the Airbus family and the achievement of the preliminary configuration freeze. Spurred on by performance shortfalls, this phase also saw some serious tweaking of the configuration. One of the most dramatic was

the decision to increase the wing size again, this time from 8,395 to 8,794 square feet.

The cross section was also improved, with a slight variation introduced into the arc size of the ovoid from forward to aft. The change was needed to increase the internal height in the aft lower cargo hold to allow one extra pair of LD3 containers to be shoe-horned into place. Further revisions were also made to the main gear, while the layout of the unusual nose area was further improved. "This was driven by one airline which wanted a seventh freight pallet in the forward hold. We had enough space for LD3s, but when we looked at pallets we saw we had some wasted space, so we did a study of extending the forward hold and moved the electronic compartment as well as part of the lower deck," explained Wissel.

The flight deck was designed from virtually the start to be on a mezzanine placed between the two main-deck levels. Together with the lower cargo hold deck, this effectively formed a four-floor arrangement that was considered best from an aerodynamic perspective, but still presented a set of unusual configuration issues.

In cross section, the revised nose layout had the look of two aircraft merged into one. The upper aircraft resembled the standard Airbus profile, and included the flight deck and crew rest areas. The lower aircraft was a massive unpressurized area, which occupied what was effectively an underhang area beneath and forward of the flight deck, and which contained the large nose undercarriage bay and the radome. The whole area was to be enclosed by a simple reinforced fairing that provided easy access for maintenance engineers.

This development phase also included efforts to reduce the area of the horizontal tailplane and vertical fin. Although necessarily very large structures, Airbus hoped to reduce their size, and therefore drag, by extensive use of a digital fly-by-wire (FBW) flight control system derived from one originally developed for the A320—the first FBW production airliner in the world. To some extent, this allowed Airbus to design the aircraft with relaxed natural aerodynamic stability, meaning that some critical flight control surfaces could be smaller and lighter than in a conventionally controlled aircraft, and yet still do the same job (see Chapter 6).

By May 1998, the design team was tackling weight issues through a series of materials changes, while the marketing team was paving the way to launch the A3XX. In light of the overall yearlong delay announced late the year before, the team had reset its sights on getting airlines on board for a possible program launch in the last quarter of 1999. This would enable entry into service about October 2004, but still required carriers to promise that they would sign on the dotted line when Airbus was in a position to offer the aircraft.

This game of chicken and egg began with Airbus seeking letters from airlines in which they would formally state their requirement for an aircraft in the A3XX category. These pledges would then be used as a form of collateral to secure a full program launch by the Airbus supervisory board in the fourth quarter of 1999. The letters would be based around the preliminary discussions held with airlines like British Airways, which had already stated a requirement for up to 23 aircraft.

But before then, Airbus faced the firm design freeze, which was needed to launch the parallel industrialization effort to actually build the aircraft. Up to 40 percent of the program was on offer to outside partners beyond the usual Airbus family, and by mid-1998 only half of this was still up for grabs. Alenia, Belairbus, Fokker Aviation (Stork), Saab Aircraft, and Finavitec had all taken early slots, being joined later in 1998 by GKN Westland Aerospace Structures of the United Kingdom and Eurocopter. Talks also continued with Aerostructures of the United States (previously a division of Textron), as well as a group of undisclosed East Asian companies.

By July 1998, the design team was defining Status 10c, a wide-ranging group of changes that included further improvements to the nose aerodynamics, particularly around the lower cheek areas on either side of the radome and above the nose gear bay.

This phase also included more changes to the shape of the rear fuselage and improvements to the empennage. Even the wing position was changed slightly, while the structure itself was refined and the overall planform improved.

Toward the end of 1998, the focus shifted to further revisions to the landing gear and rear fuselage as well as the layout of the main-deck floor. Flap track fairings were changed in profile for further drag reduction, while the wing sprouted A320-style wingtip fences. The belly fairing, until now a relatively minor feature, was also dramatically increased in size to provide drag reduction on a larger scale. Stretching from just forward of frame 33 all the way aft to beyond frame 81, the fairing ended up being over 100 feet long, or just under half the length of the entire fuselage.

The belly fairing changes were made as part of Status 10d in October 1998 and were accompanied by more alterations to the landing gear, which, for weight reasons, was looking increasingly likely to be an all-titanium design. Status 11, following that December, saw the overall dihedral, or upward sloping of the wing from the roots, reduced to about 5.6 degrees as a result of the earlier engine position change and other

The Méaulte–made flight deck structure presents an almost abstract image before work begins on completing the section of an aircraft destined for service with Australian carrier Qantas. Note the strengthened, curved nose bulkhead panel structure, painted white. The A380's large nose section, which extends below this on the finished aircraft, is unpressurized. *Mark Wagner*

decisions, while the plumbing arrangements for the outer engine fuel feed tank (No. 4) were also revised.

Another cost- and weight-saving change discussed at great length with the airlines involved reducing or eliminating the use of engine thrust reversers. As the name suggests, these devices redirect the engine power—or some of it—forward to help slow the aircraft after touchdown. Whereas some early low-bypass engines redirected all thrust by blocking the entire flow out of the exhaust, the later generation and much larger high-bypass-ratio engines deflected only the bypass stream. This limited but valuable reverse thrust was generally seen as a supplement to the stopping forces and helped reduce brake wear on landing.

In itself, cutting wear and tear on brakes was a major cost saver, and the decision to eliminate some or even all the reversers was not to be taken lightly.

Airbus canvassed airlines on the proposals about November 1998, emphasizing the potential weight saving and performance improvement from the move. In the end, a compromise was reached, and the reversers were dropped on the outside engine pair only, particularly since most airlines agreed that the increased braking thrust from the improved-efficiency engines to be used on the A3XX would help achieve a predicted stopping distance similar to, or better than, the A340, or even the 747.

The combined changes of Status 10a, b, c, and d and Status 11, and all the hard efforts of the design team were bearing fruit, and the gap to the planned performance target narrowed to within a few points. At last, after more than a year of frantic work, the teams could go back to the airlines with a much more attractive design—but they were in for a disappointment.

Market Retreat

While Airbus engineers had been working on fixing the design shortfalls of the A3XX, the prospective airline customers had been taking a financial beating. Although the worst of it had hit the Asia-Pacific market, the international nature of the airline business meant that no one escaped, wherever they were based.

The meltdown was devastating, particularly in Japan, where the two heavyweights, ANA and JAL, found themselves in the unaccustomed position of

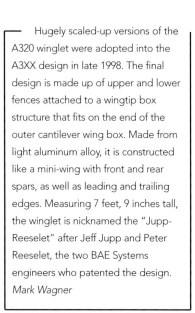

The A380 shows off its massive belly fairing during a flyover. The aerodynamic feature was dramatically extended in size in 1998, largely as a result of wind tunnel work undertaken to improve the efficiency of the A3XX. Although theoretically a secondary structure covering an area allocated mainly as housing space for the enormous undercarriage, the fairing is expected to carry some of the minor structural loads working through the interaction of the fairing substructure and the fuselage itself. *Airbus*

fighting for survival. Although both were on the A3XX design team, they were forced away from the bargaining table and began backpedaling over any potential commitments. ANA said it had "no plans to add them to our fleet, given the state of the Japanese economy." JAL said its requirement had suddenly slipped back well toward the end of the next decade. "We might feasibly have a requirement after 2010. Obviously, we are interested in a bigger aircraft . . . but, for the time being, our main concern is fixing our financial foundation, so we are having to put the brakes on investment over the next three or four years."

More worrying still, carriers such as British Airways, which had previously talked firm numbers, were now doing an about-face. The airline's chairman, Bob Ayling, had begun to talk about the growing need to compete on the basis of frequency rather than capacity, and had backed this up in late 1998 by swapping some 747 orders for the new 777. To be more flexible, and to improve yields from business traffic by increasing flights on some routes, BA was shifting its strategy away from the ultra-high-capacity concept.

The new Airbus president, Noel Forgeard, admitted that the Asian market forecast had now shrunk slightly, but he still believed an overall requirement existed for about 1,300 aircraft with a seating capacity over 400 through 2017. Of this, Airbus believed it would take a minimum of 700 orders in the category. "We have no doubts whatever on the A3XX's viability, although we are looking at slightly lower figures for the Asian market," said Forgeard, who added that the

target for launch was 30 to 40 orders from three to four customers. "We'll press the button when the market is ready and we have reasonable assurances."

Forgeard's careful words were full of foreboding for those hoping for a 1999 launch. It was not only in the market where the omens had begun to look bleak, but also in the painfully slow establishment of the new Airbus upon which the A3XX was so dependent. Talks between the partners had actually begun to lag so far behind schedule that Airbus had made the decision to officially separate the two issues. But everyone knew that, being realistic, there could be no full-scale launch of the A3XX without the formation of what was now called the single corporate entity (SCE).

Although the Boeing takeover of McDonnell Douglas in 1997 had created mounting political pressure to speed up the process, the agreement had been held up by the ongoing restructuring of the aerospace industry in Europe. In particular, the French government was grappling with the privatization of Aerospatiale and its potential merger with Dassault Aviation, and later (in 1998) the Matra Hautes Technologies group. Meanwhile Aerospatiale, caught in a difficult position facing a potential merger and restructuring at the same time, had been reluctant to reveal its valuation of its Airbus-related assets. These were extensive, with about 40 percent of its business tied up in Airbus work.

Friction between the partners continued into 1998, when the process was once again thrown off course by a proposed merger between BAe and DASA that Aerospatiale viewed as a dangerously destabiliz-

ing alliance. Despite reassurances that this was not the case, Noel Forgeard later confirmed that the restructuring was not likely until the end of 1999. But speaking at a French aviation press club meeting on November 10, he reiterated the vital need for the SCE process to go forward. "Boeing has just finished reorganizing and will seize the initiative. We must advance

at a forced march." The SCE was, he added, the only way to "reduce our production costs even more," and he reaffirmed the consortium's determination to continue. "We told the shareholders in 1996 that it would be done by 1999," he said. "We are redoubling our efforts to achieve that." He acknowledged, however, that it would more likely be at the end of the year and not the beginning.

The new performance figures Airbus revealed in April 1999 once again pointed to the vital need for the SCE. Although it had achieved record sales of $13.3 billion in 1998, Airbus had the equivalent of roughly $1.5 billion tied up in inventory. Measured in terms of stock turns—sales divided by the value of parts inventory and work in progress—the Airbus production system had slowly improved from 1.7 in 1994 to 2.9 in 1998. Airbus set a target of 4.0 for 1999, which would free $1 billion in cash.

Aircraft lead times—the period between customer specification and delivery—had fallen dramatically since 1994, from 15.5 months to 9 for the A320 family, and from 17.5 months to 1 year for the A330/A340. But the rate of progress had slowed, mired by the rigid constraints on engineering, purchasing, integration, and final assembly imposed by the Airbus structure.

Corporate confusion continued throughout Europe in early 1999 as BAe and GEC-Marconi announced a surprise merger, just as the U.K. Airbus partner was closing in on its long-negotiated deal with DASA and the formation of a European Aerospace and Defence Company (EADC). The Marconi deal sparked bitterness between the prospective Anglo-German partners and diverted DASA into the welcoming arms of newly privatized Spanish Airbus partner CASA.

The new shape of the restructured European aerospace and defense industry was slowly emerging, and with it some hope that progress toward the SCE might follow. Like some giant trees rushing down a swollen river, the new mega-companies seemed poised to break the logjam that had held up the formation of the SCE for so long. The president of the newly renamed Aerospatiale Matra, Yves Michot, agreed that "the [SCE] process has become modified mechanically" and that "we are all now talking on a bilateral basis."

Like a train gathering speed, the two-pronged movement to restructure Airbus and launch the A3XX became virtually unstoppable from 1999 onward. The Paris Air Show that year once again provided the stage to act out the latest drama. The players this time were the transport and industry ministers

from France, Germany, Spain, and the United Kingdom, who met to issue what was probably the nearest thing to an ultimatum the Airbus consortium partner companies had yet experienced. The deal was simple: come up with concrete plans to transform into an SCE or risk a clear path to research and development aid for the A3XX.

Although couched in more diplomatic language, the implicit threat was spiced up by warnings that unless Airbus got a move on, it might yet be caught by Boeing, which was quickly regaining its competitive edge after the production nightmares of the late 1990s. French transport minister Jean-Claude Gayssot said "determination was expressed very strongly" on the need "to move forward very quickly and set up the SCE for Airbus."

Gayssot added that the meeting agreed to "launch concurrently a dual effort to build the corporate entity and launch the A3XX," and said the target remained the end of 1999, with entry into service in 2005. He also revealed that the French government had "provisionally" set aside Fr200 million (U.S. $31 million) in R&D funding for the A3XX for the year. The German government position, on the other hand, remained hard-line. The German minister, Siegmar Mosdorf, said that Berlin would not budget

any money for the program without the guaranteed formation of the SCE.

But Airbus knew the frenzied rounds of mergers and privatizations throughout Europe were now all but complete, paving the way for the final round of talks between the partners. "The main handicap has been the different cultures and traditions of the European countries," said Forgeard. "The privatization of Aerospatiale is finished, and CASA is also going into the private sector, where the main focus is on shareholder value. That can only be good for the Airbus SCE process."

But just how good, not even Forgeard could have guessed. Within months, the formation of a previously unthinkable union between DaimlerChrysler Aerospace, CASA, and Aerospatiale Matra broke down the last hurdles. The old Anglo-German EADC dream was converted to a larger pan-European juggernaut dubbed the European Aeronautic Defence and Space Company (EADS), and with it the task of setting up the planned integrated company suddenly became a lot easier. Instead of four partners, there were now only two—EADS and the newly strengthened, renamed, BAE Systems.

Could the new Airbus now finally emerge, and with it the long-awaited A3XX?

When fully assembled, the massive center fuselage is the largest and most structurally complex part of the A380. Taking up the space between frames 38 and 74, the section includes passenger upper deck. The lower fuselage section includes part of the forward cargo compartment, the center wing box, the belly fairing, and the main gear bar area that houses the wing and body landing photo taken at Nantes, France. *Mark Wagner*

on the main deck, and doors 7 and 8 on the

rs. The latter area is clearly visible in this

6

High-Tech Advantage

Airbus had pushed its way into the commercial aircraft market using advanced technology as one of its trump cards. Innovation was key to differentiating its products in a market already crowded by the established American giants Boeing, Lockheed, and McDonnell Douglas.

The design team working on the selection of technologies for the A3XX therefore enjoyed a proud heritage of technological advances. With the first Airbus, the A300, they had introduced the world's first twin-engine, twin-aisle wide-body. For a 1974-vintage jetliner, it featured several new technologies, including automatic wind-shear protection, a full-flight-regime autopilot, an aft-loaded wing design, and triplex power and control systems.

In the early 1980s, Airbus followed up by introducing a raft of new flight-deck technologies that would become the standard for all future cockpits on both sides of the Atlantic. The A300FF (forward-facing) cockpit was the first to automate the flight engineer's tasks and to introduce a computer-based digital flight management system to reduce pilot workload. For the first time, pilots were introduced to a dark, quiet flight deck in which any system not activated or switched off would be conspicuous because the light would show in a dark panel. It was the start of a display philosophy that was essentially based around the theme of "don't distract the crew with something until they need to know it."

Airbus took this philosophy to the next logical step with the A310 in 1983, when it introduced cathode ray tube–based flight instruments and an electronic centralized aircraft

monitor display. The same aircraft was also used as the platform for two other hallmark Airbus technological innovations: large-scale composites and fly-by-wire flight control. Although the A310 was just a stepping stone toward much fuller implementation of these advances in later aircraft, it was the first to have carbon-fiber–reinforced plastic (CFRP) used in aerodynamic fairings, and the first to use electrically signaled flaps, slats, and spoilers.

The A310-300 in 1985 took these on another great leap when CFRP was used for the first time in a major primary structure, in this case the fin box. Taking a leaf out of the Concorde design book, the -300 also introduced the subsonic world to the use of tailplane trim tanks for controlling the center of gravity.

But arguably it was with the A320 in 1988 that Airbus really gained its global reputation as an innovator. The consortium's first narrow-body faced entrenched challengers in the form of the best-selling 737 and MD-80 families, and was therefore packed to the hilt with new game-changing technology. For the first time on any commercial airliner, the A320 featured digital fly-by-wire flight controls and active ailerons. On the flight deck it had side stick controllers that seemed more familiar to F-16 pilots and computer game players than to commercial air crew. The side sticks controlled pitch and roll, with an automatic system for pitch trim. Structurally as well, the

A320 was highly advanced, with a greater proportion of composites than anything before it. Combining previous lessons from developing the A310, the A320 not only used CFRP in the ailerons, spoilers, and elevators, but also in the tailplane and fin as well.

Similar evolutionary developments emerged on the A330/A340, which in most cases saw their use on a much larger scale. From an innovation perspective, however, the larger quad and twin family were most important for having a common cockpit, which not only enabled crews to fly either the A330 or A340, but also the A320 series. The so-called cross-crew-qualification feature would prove to be a winning formula in sales battles to come, and a vital weapon in the growing war with Boeing for market share. The later A340-500/600 also provided an opening for a materials innovation in the form of thermoplastics, which were used for the first time to form the wing leading-edge J-nose.

So while top management, accountants, and lawyers struggled through the complexities of forming the SCE, the growing team of engineers and designers continued to battle the equally daunting challenges of weight and cost targets for the A3XX as the final design freeze loomed. It now became clearer which key innovations would be at the forefront.

Alloys and Composites

By late 1999 and early 2000, an estimated 40 percent of the A3XX structure and components were to be made from carbon composites and advanced metal alloys. The design by now finally incorporated a one-piece wing structure with a carbon-fiber wing box, the first in any commercial aircraft. The use of composites saved up to a ton and a half compared to using the most advanced aluminum alloys, said Airbus. A monolithic CFRP design was also adopted for the fin box and rudder, as well as the massive horizontal stabilizer and elevators.

Inside the fuselage, the upper-deck floor beams and, surprisingly to some outsiders, the pressure bulkheads were also to be made of CFRP. At this stage the wing skins were still expected to be made of advanced aluminum alloys, though here again composites soon took over. The fixed-wing leading edges, on the other hand, were to be made from thermoplastics, while the secondary support structure holding the interior furnishing and cabin trim in place were expected to be made from the same materials. Further potential applications of thermoplastics included ribs in the fixed leading edges of the vertical and horizontal stabilizers.

Glare

To save weight, a material called GLARE was chosen in late 1999 for the upper fuselage shell of the A3XX. GLARE (glass-fiber–reinforced aluminum laminate) was tested as early as 1990 in evaluations by Delft University and the Netherlands National Aerospace Laboratory, along with Aerospatiale, Deutsche Airbus, and original GLARE maker AKZO (which later became Fokker Aerostructures Structural Laminates Industries before becoming Stork Aerospace). The material consisted of alternating layers of four or more 0.015-inch (0.38-millimeter) aluminum sheets and glass-fiber–reinforced bond film and was 10 percent less dense than aluminum. The material thickness could be changed by adding sheets to match the local load requirements, while the glass fiber served as both a load path and crack-stopper between the aluminum sheets. Offering a weight saving of 15 to 30 percent over aluminum, the material was tested on an A330/A340 fuselage barrel and had been considered for possible use in the A321.

Flight tests were also conducted from the second half of 1999 onward on a German Air Force A310 multi-role transport, which was fitted with a 12-foot-by-4-foot,-11-inch panel between frames 35 and 40 and stringers 5 and 13 on the right forward fuselage. The modification was completed by Lufthansa Technik with DaimlerChrysler Aerospace Airbus and was certified by Germany's civil aviation authority. By mid-2000, Airbus estimated that it would save about

The A310 was used to introduce successive waves of innovations. When it entered the market in 1983, the baseline model brought with it cathode ray tube–based flight instruments; electronic centralized aircraft monitor displays; CFRP secondary structures; and electrically signaled flaps, slats, and spoilers. The A310-300, one of which is pictured here over the beach at St. Maarten in the Caribbean, added even more features two years later. The most important of these included a carbon composite–based fin and tailplane, the first ever use of CFRP in primary structure, and the use of tailplane trim tanks for center of gravity control. In one way or another, all these elements would later find their way into the A380. *Mark Wagner*

1,760 pounds on the A3XX, as well as having better corrosion, fatigue-, and damage- resistance properties.

Laser-beam Welding

An advanced manufacturing process developed to speed up assembly as well as reduce weight was laser-beam welding (LBW), which would be used to attach the stringers of the lower fuselage shell skins. The same process, which could weld up to 26 feet of stringers per minute, cut weight by reducing the amount of weld material used and included a built-in automated inspection unit. It also eliminated fasteners, which are a major source of corrosion and fatigue cracks. So promising was the process that it was introduced into the assembly line as early as 2001 to make the fuselage lower skin panels of the A318, with other applications to follow. LBW was also proposed for use on the curved, pressurized bulkhead below the flight deck floor.

High-pressure Hydraulics

Tests in early 1999 showed that empty weight could be trimmed by about 1 metric ton by using a new higher-pressure hydraulic system running at 5,000 psi

(345 bar), or about one-third higher than contemporary conventional aircraft systems. All-electric actuators, which would have been powered by locally generated hydraulic pressure, had by now been rejected because of insufficient maturity for the loads required. "The main landing gear will weigh more than 44,050 pounds, for example," said Robert Lafontan, A380 senior vice president for engineering.

The final design was a partially decentralized system that included a local hydraulic reservoir for a series of electro-hydraulic actuators and saved an estimated 2,200 pounds overall. The final design would incorporate a remarkable network of tubes and pipes stretching over 3,300 feet.

Air Generation

Faced with maintaining just the right cabin atmosphere for a space that could accommodate up to 840 passengers, Airbus scoured the industry for the most powerful environmental control system (ECS) ever conceived. The chosen system, which Hamilton Sundstrand eventually selected for development (see Chapter 7), was a double-spool, air-generating system that promised better thermodynamic efficiency, occupied less volume, and offered more redundancy. Instead of opting for the conventional air conditioning system approach, in which high-temperature, low-pressure bleed air from the engine compressor stages is converted to pressurized cabin air at room temperatures, the A3XX was to have two innovative double-packs. Each pack contained four air cycle machines, each of which had four stages, and were 85 percent more powerful than any previous ECS developed by the company. Each unit performed separate functions within the overall cycle.

Flight Control System

By June 1999, flight tests had also begun of an A340 fitted with a reduced-stability configuration as part of efforts to validate the technology for the A3XX. Natural stability was reduced by transferring fuel between tanks so the aircraft's center of gravity was moved aft. This meant that the aircraft was more finely balanced and required less downward force to be applied by the horizontal tailplane for stability. By using a high-fidelity FBW flight control system, Airbus believed it could take maximum benefit from the move by reducing the size of the 2,580-square-foot tailplane by up to 10 percent, to approximately 2,153 square feet. This could reduce trim drag by about 0.5 percent and save 1,500 pounds in weight, directly contributing to overall operating cost reduction.

The center wing box is one of the most massive single-structural elements in the A380 and extends across the width of the fuselage. Split into two cells, the box can be used as a fuel tank depending on the version, though the A380-800 will not use this feature and therefore has a dry center wing box. Composite materials are used throughout the structure for the spars, upper and lower skin panels, and stiffeners. The diagonally orientated struts support the floor structure above as seen in this wing box being built in Nantes for an Emirates aircraft. *Mark Wagner*

Advanced automated laser-beam welding techniques produce the lower fuselage skin panels below the main deck floor level, as well as the curved bulkhead panel below the flight deck. With this process, either a carbon dioxide or solid-state YAG (yttrium-aluminum-garnet) laser welds the stringers to the skin. *Airbus*

So far everyone involved in the A3XX had been forced to use their imagination to judge the true scale of what they were involved in, be they engineers, designers, suppliers, or airlines. Now, as the winter of 1999–2000 approached, this was about to change as the first huge A3XX mockup sections started arriving by truck at Toulouse. Made by a local supplier, Sefca-Queutelot, the initial mockup was the upper-deck section only, but would later be extended to provide a full-length, full-diameter representative cross section, including main deck and lower cargo hold.

The section, installed in a new mockup center adjacent to the Airbus headquarters building at Toulouse, gave airline customers in particular a real-life impression of what they were being offered or what they had already bought. Various interiors and features, some of them future options not yet finalized, would also be displayed among the mockup collection, which eventually included the A300-600, A330-200, A340-600, and the narrow-body A319, A320, and A321.

Aware of the need to keep the momentum going, the supervisory board meanwhile met across the road from the mockup center at an extraordinary meeting in early December. The board authorized Managing Director Noel Forgeard to begin touring airlines to ask them to sign letters of support to gauge market demand. Assuming that sufficient commitments could be obtained, the outline plan was to expedite the delayed A3XX schedule and target mid-2000 for the commercial launch.

Some, however, were reading the omens in a completely different way. For example, a U.S. consultancy, the Teal Group, announced a pessimistic 10-year delivery forecast in early 2000, predicting slack demand for the A3XX size category until 2009—and even then saying that a mere six aircraft would be required! Beyond this, the Teal Group saw a slow, steady demand for three aircraft per month over subsequent years. Airbus immediately rejected the forecast, pointing out that some of the oldest 747-400s would be 15 to 16 years old by 2005, making them ripe for replacement.

The airline response to the first major sales foray was encouraging, but SIA and Qantas were adamant about needing an additional range of 300 to 400 nautical miles. "SIA needed to reach London, of course, and Qantas wanted transpacific range," said Airbus Marketing Vice President Colin Stuart. "SIA also wanted QC/2 [the emerging new tough nighttime-noise requirement at London Heathrow]. Until then we weren't guaranteeing QC/2. We targeted it, but SIA wanted it guaranteed. It therefore became a directive from Forgeard that we had to have these things in order to launch."

Stuart recalled that at that meeting both the range improvement (finally agreed on at 350 nautical miles) and the requirement to meet QC/2 rules became pivotal conditions for launch. But how could the A3XX meet QC/2? Tests and predictions increasingly showed that the giant jetliner was marginal at best, and Airbus decided that it had to bite the bullet

With the 5,000-psi hydraulic system unpowered, the enormous elevators and ailerons of the A380 are at rest. The use of the advanced Eaton-developed hydraulic system—which still uses the industry-standard ester-phosphate–based fluid—saved about 2,645 pounds in weight, and eased maintenance concerns.
Mark Wagner

Although the 1990s had turned out to be a difficult time to launch the double-decker, the culmination of the decade was a watershed time for Airbus and its dream of market parity with Boeing. As the 1999 numbers were tallied, it became clear that Airbus had not only completely outsold its rival, but had also ended the year with a massive 48 percent of the total number of undelivered new airliners held in the firm order backlog. What better omens could there be as Forgeard headed out on his quest for signed letters of support?

When the wing is joined to the fuselage, the deep, open area in the leading-edge root between the fuselage and the inboard part of the wing housing, the "droop nose," is faired over and used to house the double air conditioning packs that Hamilton Sundstrand produces. The root chord of the wing, or the distance from the leading to trailing edge measured parallel to the longitudinal axis, is an astonishing 58 feet!
Mark Wagner

and immediately build in greater takeoff noise margin. The package of changes included a significant series of engine modifications to increase bypass ratio and reduce noise emissions, as well as the knock-on effects of drag and weight (see Chapter 10).

To improve the lift/drag ratio by 5 percent, mostly for takeoff and initial climb, the wing design was changed to incorporate a droop-nose device by the inboard leading edge. This variable-position device, similar in design to one developed for the Hawker Siddeley Trident, was used instead of a more conventional Kruger flap because of the sheer depth of the giant wing root. The droop device was a masterpiece of design to solve a difficult problem, according to Frank Ogilvie, A380 aerodynamics director and deputy head of the overall aircraft design.

"One of the thoughts was to go to a completely sealed slat system, but we couldn't do that because Boeing has the design rights," Ogilvie said. "Also, the wing was still stalling between the engines and not near the root, so the question was, how could we do a sealed slat that wasn't sealed? In the end, British Aerospace at Filton came up with the drooped nose idea. The beauty about the design is that it is always sealed as the rotating part is within the profile of the wing. In high-lift configuration, it meets the require-

ment for maximum lift but has substantially better drag. It also allows the wing to stall inboard, because it does not have a slot."

The ailerons were also rigged to droop at takeoff, adding to the overall lift. The flight management system was optimized for improved takeoff and noise abatement procedures. The changes, added to the range increase, resulted in a total weight impact of about 26,000 pounds, which was reflected in a decision to increase the highest maximum takeoff weight option from 1.207 to 1.233 million pounds. The increases in engine size and acoustic treatments, for example, result-

For takeoff, the trailing-edge high-lift system is made up of primarily the three single-slotted flap sections on each wing, seen clearly in this view of MSN001. To further improve takeoff performance and guarantee meeting London Heathrow's stringent QC/2 noise rules, the design team rigged the ailerons to droop for takeoff. The aileron is divided into three segments and provides valuable additional outboard lift in this "move down" configuration. *Mark Wagner*

ed in an overall weight increase of about 6,600 pounds and led to the further extension of advanced alloys, composites, and thermoplastics in the wings.

Many of these changes were still being finalized at the time of the 2000 Asian Aerospace show in Singapore, where Airbus vice president for A3XX market development, Philippe Jarry, was busy reassuring airlines that the aircraft would still be a wonderful performer. Despite the recent pessimistic Teal forecast, Jarry also said, "You have airlines that have a policy of replacing their aircraft early, so we believe 2005 is in line with market requirements." He did add, however, that airlines had shown zero interest in the proposed 480-seat A3XX-50R shrink. It also emerged that hopes remained high of launching both the baseline -100 passenger and -100F freighter variants simultaneously at the end of the year, even though the cargo version would not enter service until 2007.

Outline proposals were handed out to the airlines, with Cathay Pacific, MAS, and SIA being offered deals of between 12 and 15 aircraft each. Discussions were also underway on the A3XX-100F with Emirates, United, and Virgin Atlantic, as well as with the big cargo carriers, including Atlas Air, Cargolux, Lufthansa Cargo, and FedEx.

The massive sales push was tactical as well as strategic. Most of the target carriers were already members of one of the powerful new airline groups such as oneworld, SkyTeam, and the Star Alliance. As key members of a larger group, any airline that committed to the A3XX would therefore exert a strong influence on other partners in terms of new aircraft.

Mike Turner, chief operating officer of BAE Systems, said that it was more important to secure "a range of major airline customers covering all the major global alliances," than it was to rack up a specific tally of aircraft orders. Penetration of the four major alliances was vital. "If we can secure a first wave of major customers, we would expect other airlines to follow," said Turner. Significant discounts were offered as an incentive to the first takers. Depending on options and interior configurations, the official list price for the A3XX-100 varied from $218 to $240 million, while the stretched -200 was priced between $244 and $253 million.

Gathering Inertia

The airline response to the first major sales foray was encouraging and was enough for Airbus to pencil in May 26 as the date for a go/no-go decision on the commercial launch of the A3XX. Philippe Camus, president of Aerospatiale Matra, said that the decision would depend on "not only straight numbers, but the quality of the customers, the potential of the A3XX to satisfy demand from global alliances, and the suitability of airports."

The launch, should it come, meant that a full industrial launch would follow in December, with delivery of the first aircraft toward the end of 2005. But who would that first customer be? Despite all the focus on the big-name airlines such as Cathay Pacific, Qantas, SIA, United, and Virgin, it was something of a surprise when, in late April 2000, it was the rapidly growing Dubai-based airline Emirates that first emerged as a potential buyer.

The news had leaked out, and was not officially confirmed by Airbus, which remained tight-lipped. Emirates would only say it had officially notified the manufacturer of its intent to order five A3XXs and place five options should the program be launched. Two further A3XX-100Fs were also tentatively added to the mix. Then, within weeks of the planned critical May meeting, SIA quietly followed Emirates by signing a letter expressing interest in up to 10 A3XXs. Airbus later confirmed SIA was in discussion for 10 firm and six option A3XXs for delivery from 2005, although the final deal announced at the end of that September for up to 25 aircraft was bigger than anyone at Airbus could have hoped for.

Why the secrecy? SIA was traditionally a cautious, conservative carrier and was carefully considering its options, which, at this point, still included a potential 747X offering from Boeing. The airline had gained massive strength in its global network on the back of the 747 and had even taken delivery of the 1,000th aircraft produced by Boeing. SIA was also a major 777 customer and enjoyed close links with the U.S. manufacturer, which had offered it a deal covering six firm -400X and nine options as a possible bridge to a stretched 747X variant.

Boeing had by now stepped up efforts to promote the higher gross weight 910,000-pound takeoff -400X, and planned a seminar for potential customers—including Cathay Pacific and SIA—in June. The -400X was a vital part of a revised Boeing strategy to try and counter the A3XX with a renewed attempt to develop a stretch 747. This time, Boeing was trying a building-block approach, with the first step on the ladder being the -400IGW (increased gross weight) variant, which was first proposed in 1997. (The -400IGW was later renamed the -400X and ultimately became the -400ER when launched with an order by Qantas for six passenger versions in November 2000.)

The heavier-weight version was beefed up to offer longer range, and provided the structural foundations for two potential stretch versions. Originally, Boeing saw the first of these being the -400Y, featuring a wing root insert and a stretched fuselage with seats for an extra 70 passengers. A longer-range version of the -400Y was also contemplated, but with the original -400X fuselage length.

The airlines remained cool to the Boeing plan, so a more radical revamp was designed, but still using the -400X as a foundation. The stretched version again featured a wing root insert that extended wing span to 230 feet and increased fuselage length by 31.5 feet. Maximum takeoff weight was increased to 1.043 million pounds, and up to 100 more seats could be fitted. The aircraft would, said Boeing, have up to 545 nautical miles more range and about 10 percent lower

Emirates surprised the aerospace world, and possibly even Airbus, by becoming the largest customer for the aircraft with orders of 43 aircraft by mid-2005, almost one-third of the total orders. The airline, which wanted the superjumbo to boost the capacity of its Dubai–based hub operations from 2008 onward, leased two additional aircraft from ILFC to ensure it met its requirements. The airline would be the first to operate the A380 in the region that expected massive growth in the decade to come. In 2004, 21.7 million passengers passed through Dubai; this number was expected to mushroom to about 60 million by 2010. *Mark Wagner*

An early A3XX configuration model shows the aircraft before its final series of "Status" improvements. Note the additional upper deck forward exit, the broad chord of the horizontal tail, and the relatively small aerodynamic fairing around the wing to body join. *Mark Wagner*

The intense debate over where to place the A3XX final assembly site was finally boiled down to two sites, Toulouse and Hamburg. The Toulouse site, adjacent to Blagnac Airport, was the traditional home of Airbus assembly since the 1970s, but DASA had made a strong case for the A3XX, having recently modernized its Hamburg facilities to assemble the A319 and A321 variants of the A320 family. The Toulouse bid involved the construction of massive new facilities on the north side of the field, well away from the existing production site and the then-new Clement-Ader A330/A340 assembly building, which was four years old when this photo was taken in 1994. The complete site at that time covered 130 acres and was named after the Frenchman who, in 1890, had made a brief hop in a steam-powered, bat-winged "aeroplane." *Mark Wagner*

seat–mile costs. It was also to be offered with derivatives of the Engine Alliance GP7000 engines in development for the A3XX, or a new variant of the Rolls-Royce Trent family dubbed the 600.

The newest stretch study was based around a 777-style wing root section, simpler double-slotted flaps, drooped ailerons for takeoff, and a trailing-edge wedge design, originally conceived by McDonnell Douglas, on the outboard wing only. The same features would also be used on a shorter-fuselage version that would be derived from the 747S Stretch and resemble the standard -400 in length and passenger capacity. But by using the bigger wing, improved aerodynamics, and engines of the larger Stretch, the new 747X would become the world's longest-range aircraft, capable of flying up to 442 passengers across a range of 8,975 nautical miles.

Armed with performance data that said the 747X Stretch would beat the projected operating costs of the A3XX-100, a high-powered Boeing team hit the boardrooms of the major Asia-Pacific carriers in the crucial few weeks before the Airbus meeting in May. The team included the experienced Boeing Product Strategy and Development Vice President John Roundhill and Joe Sutter, the mercurial father of the 747. To prepare the airlines for their visit, Boeing Chairman and Chief Executive Phil Condit had even sent each a letter exhorting the airlines not to commit to the big Airbus until they could be fully briefed on the final performance estimates of the 747X.

The effort did succeed in establishing the launch of the -400ER, which went on to be ordered as both a passenger and a freight aircraft, but it could not stop the inexorable progress of the A3XX toward launch.

As it turned out, however, the big Airbus May 26 go-ahead meeting to give the project the official green light was postponed, but not because of the Boeing counterattack, said Airbus. Rather, the consortium said that extra time was needed to fine-tune other aspects of the program, particularly final decisions over funding, allocations of work share, and the location of the final assembly line. Airbus hoped to hold the meeting at the upcoming Berlin Air Show on June 8.

Finding enough money was crucial for Airbus. Camus said that the Airbus partners were spending Fr250 million (U.S. $42 million) each month on the A3XX effort and were effectively "working in a world in which it is already launched." The program had been getting some good news on this front, however. While Forgeard had been on his sales road trip, the first state-aid grant for the 3XX program, now valued at about $12 billion, was announced by the U.K. government, which approved an $835 million (£530 million) loan to BAE Systems. The move inevitably sparked complaints from Boeing that, over the subsequent years, would eventually reignite the furious transatlantic dispute over subsidies that had only been grudgingly settled under the provisions of a 1992 trade agreement (see Chapter 13).

News of the loan also came as the Airbus partners finally reached unofficial agreement to house the A3XX final assembly line in Toulouse, France. The rumors leaking out of Airbus suggested that the agreement covered an overall rationalization of the production setup, with Toulouse taking the lead on all widebody production, and Hamburg assuming final assembly of all single-aisle aircraft. The truth, when it came out, was more complex and somewhat unexpected (see Chapter 8).

Customer momentum was simultaneously building, with Air France becoming the next airline to join the potential launch group with a requirement of up to 10 new aircraft. In early June, Air France's president, Jean-Cyril Spinetta, said that the A3XX, "could constitute the appropriate solution for Air France in the very-large-capacity market, meeting our needs in terms of capacity for the projected growth in air traffic, but also in terms of range, operational efficiency, passenger comfort, and environmental friendliness."

A week later, Emirates Chief Maurice Flanagan was more vocal in his support when he wrote a letter to London's Evening Standard newspaper saying, "With world passenger numbers growing at 5 percent a year, I don't know what other airlines are waiting for. Takeoff and landing slots at major airports will continue to be tight and we will need bigger aircraft."

Meanwhile, talks to create the new Airbus, now dubbed the Airbus Integrated Company (AIC), stormed ahead between BAE and the soon-to-be-formed EADS companies, though several major issues remained to be solved, including financial share and corporate governance. Although the issues of the AIC and the A3XX launch were officially separated, the two were inevitably linked, and by June 2000 the partners agreed to sort out both issues at the same time. In theory, the AIC and A3XX could not be tied directly because talks over the formation of the "new" Airbus were going on at partner level, while authority to offer

the A3XX rested with the Airbus supervisory board. The building blocks of the AIC were completed when the last hurdles were cleared for the formation of EADS with the merger of Aerospatiale Matra, CASA, and DaimlerChrysler Aerospace.

The basic framework of the AIC divided ownership between EADS, with 80 percent, and BAE Systems, with 20 percent. The company was to be registered in France and was expected to produce almost immediate savings by allowing the partners to streamline procurement, eliminate duplication, and reduce production overheads. Overall, EADS predicted savings of up to €350 million (U.S. $407 million) by 2004. Employing about 41,500 people, the AIC was to be governed by a seven-member shareholder committee, with five representatives from EADS and two from BAE. Rainer Hertrich, co-chief executive of EADS, would be chairman while the day-to-day management would be headed by Forgeard.

In an interview with the French newspaper Le Monde on June 14, 2000, Forgeard described the talks between BAE Systems and the newly created EADS as going well. As for the commercial launch decision, which now seemed to be subject to one embarrassing holdup after another, he said, "there is no reason to delay further. From now on, Airbus' credibility as well as my own is at stake."

The reorganization of Airbus into a single corporate entity, the new Airbus Integrated Company (AIC), was pivotal to the go-ahead of the A380 and was finally achieved in June 2000 after years of negotiation and a flurry of mergers. The partners were made up of EADS with 80 percent and BAE Systems with 20 percent. *Mark Wagner*

Although Emirates is credited with the first official firm order for the A380, it was Virgin Atlantic's $3.8 billion order for six aircraft in December 2000 that took the firm order book through the 50 its approval for the launch of the project. *Airbus*

...llowing the Airbus supervisory board to give

7

Enter the A380 Superjumbo

On December 19, 2000, the news the industry was waiting for finally broke—the Airbus supervisory board had voted to launch the A380, the new name for the A3XX.

But why A380, rather than A350 or A360, both of which had been the next logical designations in the Airbus numbering system? Although the use of the numeral 8 was already believed to be good luck to many Asian cultures, and therefore a consideration toward the large customer base of the region, Forgeard said the final designation was selected because "8 suggests double-decks, one on top of the other."

The first variant was therefore to be the A380-800, replacing the A3XX-100, while the reduced-capacity 480-seater variant previously dubbed the A3XX-50R was renamed the A380-700. The stretched A3XX-200 was now known as the A380-900, while a longer-range derivative of the baseline A3XX-100 was to be called the A380-800R, and the freighter version the -800F.

Then there was the question of using the higher-end -700/-800/-900 designations for the derivatives straight out of the box. Airbus Chief Commercial Officer John Leahy said that this approach was taken because the three versions were fully developed aircraft and the -100/-200/-300 designations would be subject to earlier obsolescence and therefore lower residual values.

Manfred Bischoff, chairman of the Airbus supervisory board and EADS co-chairman, said, "Airbus has a new flagship. This is a major breakthrough for Airbus as a full-range competitor on world markets. We are convinced that this aircraft will have a bright and extremely successful future. It will be proof of the outstanding capabilities and skills of

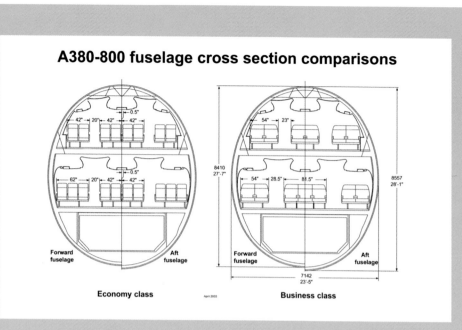

A380-800 fuselage cross section comparisons

Economy class

Forward fuselage · Aft fuselage

Business class

Forward fuselage · Aft fuselage

8410 27'-7"
8557 28'-1"
7142 23'-5"

April 2003

Europe's aerospace industry and represents a completely new generation of technology in the field of aircraft manufacturing and air travel. I am personally very proud and happy to give the go-ahead for a project that I fought for since 1989."

Forgeard—the credibility of both Airbus and himself now ensured—was also in a fulsome mood. "This decision crowns the efforts of all those who have worked so hard on the project for the last four years, and in particular the 20 airlines and 50 airports, the airworthiness authorities, engine manufacturers, suppliers, industrial partners, and not least, our shareholders and all the Airbus staff, whose dedication helped shape the program and bring it to fruition."

Forgeard left his last comment for perhaps the most important players in this chapter of the A380 story—the six launch customers to whom he extended "my warmest congratulations."

The group included SIA, Emirates, the leasing giant International Lease Finance Company (ILFC), Qantas, Air France, and Virgin—the latter's $3.8 bil-

The additional cross-sectional area of the aft fuselage resulted primarily from the requirements of some prime launch candidate carriers such as Singapore Airlines for increased lower cargo deck capacity and was a key element of the final pre-launch design refinements in 2000 to increase range and meet London QC/2 noise goals.

Australian flag carrier Qantas joined the launch party with an order and options for up to 24 aircraft. The airline planned to configure its aircraft in a three-class, 501-seat layout on transpacific services from Australia to the United States, and on its Kangaroo Route from Australia to the United Kingdom. The airline planned to deploy four A380-800s on the services to the United States and expected to be the first carrier to operate services to that country with the new Airbus. *Airbus*

lion order for six in December being the final breakthrough needed to achieve Airbus's 50-order target. The Virgin deal, announced just four days before the final go-ahead, included initial deliveries from 2006 and was part of the airline's strategy to expand its existing trunk routes as well as add new services. The airline's ebullient chairman, Sir Richard Branson, said, "I am incredibly excited about the opportunities these aircraft will bring—our reputation has been built on innovation and the A3XX will give us the opportunity to create a new flying experience for our passengers."

The new interior configuration of its recently ordered A340-600s, featuring stand-up bars and the provision for massage stations on its 747s, underlined the willingness of Virgin to operate out of the box, with the A380 providing the massive scope for never-before-seen features on modern aircraft. Although Airbus was keen to market the potential for bars, libraries, gyms, and even showers, it wasn't clear how many, if any, of these would actually take flight. Cheong Choong Kong, deputy chairman and chief executive of SIA, which was also a 49 percent stake-

holder in Virgin, said the A380 would allow the potential for "service innovations and unprecedented levels of comfort." He admitted, however, that the airline would be reluctant to give up revenue-earning seats for what he termed as flights of fantasy features.

Qantas had also added its considerable force to the prelaunch momentum in December 2000 by placing orders and options for up to 24 aircraft. The deal, worth a massive $4.6 billion, also included A330s and the launch order for the 747-400ER, although the latter was widely considered something of a consolation prize to Boeing, which had worked hard on the

the dotted line early in 2001 would probably benefit from a similar introductory offer. "We'll probably say okay to them as well—it's in the business case (for acceptable pricing for launch customers)."

Airbus also took the opportunity during the industrial launch of the A380 to make significant changes within its top management team, just as the company began its official transition to AIC. The biggest move was the appointment of Charles Champion as senior vice president of the A380 program. An aerospace engineer with a master's degree from Stanford University who had begun with Aerospatiale's Airbus division in 1979, Champion came from the single-aisle A320-family program where he had led the effort to ramp up production to an unprecedented 23 aircraft per month. He had also had stints with sales for southeast Europe and the CIS, as well as managing director of the Airbus Military Company, which was being set up to develop the A400M airlifter. Champion, then 45 years old, had led the A400M through the ups and downs of five years of prelaunch development, and had taken over from J,rgen Thomas, who had stepped down from the project to become special advisor to Forgeard.

Almost immediately, Champion invoked changes in the structure to see the A380 into production. Aircraft component management teams (ACMTs), tasked with engineering, manufacturing, and product support, were co-located at Airbus sites around Europe. "It is the first time we have co-located teams for a new aircraft program," said Champion, who promised that the first work packages would be signed within weeks. ACMTs were devised for the wing, nose, center fuselage, forward and aft fuselage, propulsion, empennage, landing gear, systems, interior, and final assembly line (FAL).

Each ACMT acted like a mini-program of its own, with a head overseeing program management, engineering, industrial, procurement, quality, and customer services. Within each ACMT were several combined design build teams (CDBTs) with specific responsibility for sub-elements. ACMT allocation was related to the traditional Airbus center-of-excellence philosophy, with responsibility for the nose and center fuselage being taken by Airbus France,

Charles Champion, the youthful executive vice president of the A380, was appointed to lead the mammoth development effort once it transitioned from the A3XX. He is pictured, in a blue tie, with the triumphant flight test crew after the completion of the maiden flight on April 27, 2005. To his left, also wearing a suit, is Airbus Chief Executive Noel Forgeard. *Mark Wagner*

A wing during assembly before equipping has begun. Assembly of major components of the aircraft was divided into aircraft component management teams (ACMTs), with each team representing a mini version of the entire project. Wing assembly, for example, was headquartered at Airbus U.K. in Filton with major construction work undertaken at a specially built site at Broughton on the Welsh border. *Mark Wagner*

Australian campaign as hopes of finding a strong 747X Stretch candidate in the Asia-Pacific market had begun to narrow to just Cathay Pacific and Korean Air.

Like the other launch customers, Qantas had benefited from a roughly 30 percent discount on the A380 list price of $230 million. Philippe Jarry commented that follow-on customers lining up to sign on

forward and aft fuselage by Airbus Germany, the wings by Airbus U.K., tail cone and empennage by Airbus Spain, and wing leading edges by Belairbus of Belgium.

Despite the fact that suppliers and risk-sharing partners rapidly were being selected, some key design decisions were still undecided. One of these, only recently finalized, was the decision to go to an all-

Qatar Airways was scheduled to take delivery of the first of up to four A380-800s in 2009 to coincide with the opening of the new Doha International Airport, the first in the world to be designed and built specifically to take the double-decker. The new airport site, 40 percent of which was reclaimed from the Arabian Gulf, cost $2.5 billion to develop during the first phase, making it capable of handling 12 million passengers a year. The second phase, taking it through to 2015, will expand capacity to 50 million passengers at a cost of $5.5 billion. *Airbus*

The air traffic meltdown after the September 11, 2001, terrorist attacks on the United States delayed Lufthansa's December 2001 order for 15 firm and six A380 options. It planned to freeze its configuration in October 2005 and make a final decision on the exterior paintwork in June 2006. Deliveries were expected to begin late in 2007 with the first batch of four in service by the spring of 2008. *Airbus*

The 22 wheels of the undercarriage are clearly visible from below for the first time as the A380 takes off to start its test career. The body landing gear, consisting of a six-wheel bogie, retracts aft while the wing landing gear has a four-wheel bogie and retracts sideways into the belly fairing. The United Kingdom–based landing gear supplier, ACMT, brought together nose gear components from Messier-Dowty in France, Goodrich body and main gear from the United States and Canada, wheels and brakes from Honeywell and Dunlop in the United States, and tires from Michelin in France and Bridgestone in Japan. Messier Bugatti of France also supplied the braking and steering system, while Smiths of the United Kingdom provided the retraction and extension system and Eldec of the United States, the sensors. *Mark Wagner*

The sophisticated interactive displays and integrated avionics of the A380 flight deck are connected by a Rockwell Collins–supplied avionics full duplex (AFDX) Ethernet-switched data link, providing 100 Mbit/s two-way communications among the flight controls, navigation and radio systems, engines, flight deck, and the many utility systems (see Chapter 12). The system is mainly used for data file transfer and incorporates safeguards to ensure messages are partitioned and do not get jumbled or go to the wrong "subscriber." Although the overhead panel layout differs slightly from previous Airbus cockpits, the "dark cockpit" philosophy of the A320 is retained with pushbuttons remaining unlit if everything is working normally. *Mark Wagner*

metallic wing, rather than attempting to make the outer sections from composite materials. Although this had offered the tantalizing weight saving of up to 3,080 pounds per ship set, a fuller analysis showed that the final weight saving would have been eroded by the need for a massive structural join between the two sections where the inboard metal structure attached to the carbon-fiber–reinforced plastic (CFRP) outer third of the wing. Added weight would have also been incurred through the need to strengthen the wing to counter the loss of bending relief moment from the lighter structure. Added together, the "plastic" wing ended up bringing in a weight savings of less than 1,500 pounds, which Airbus decided was simply not worth the higher manufacturing costs.

Sales of the A380 meanwhile appeared to be on a roll during the first year and were forecast by John Leahy to break the 100 barrier by the end of 2001. In particular, talks with freight operators were well-advanced, he said, and it was a deal with parcel carrier FedEx for 10 A380-800Fs that took the tally to 97, along with 59 options, by the end of December 2001. In late February 2001, Qatar Airways became a surprise ninth firm customer for the giant jetliner, and the third freighter operator after FedEx and Emirates (which had ordered two) with an order for two plus two options. The order came as part of a bigger deal including A330s.

Others placing orders in 2001 included Lufthansa, which signed for 15. The aircraft "could be used for daily flights from Frankfurt to New Delhi, New York, Tokyo, and Singapore," said Lufthansa, which, despite officially opting for the A380, still kept the door open for a later 747X buy. The official signing for the A380s could not be firmed up, however, until a wage dispute was settled with the Vereinigung Cockpit German pilots union. It was then further delayed by the airline's decision to hold off from all major aircraft purchases following the September 11 terrorist attacks on the United States before finally being ratified in December.

Supplier Selection Starts

As the program entered its first full year as the A380, the major suppliers began to line up for work. The U.S.–based undercarriage maker BF Goodrich (later simply Goodrich) was selected early in 2001 to supply the body and wing gear in a deal potentially worth $2 to $3 billion over the first 20 years. Goodrich, which also provided the gear for the 747 and 777, beat off competition from Messier-Dowty, which nonetheless won the contract for the hefty forward landing gear.

The massive six-wheel body gear, similar in overall appearance to the 777 main gear, weighed in at more than 8,970 pounds compared to about 3,000 pounds for the stockier four-wheel body gear on the 747. The four-wheeled wing gear, by contrast, was expected to weigh about 5,100 pounds compared to the 3,890-pound 747 gear. Under the deal, which was its first main gear contract for any Airbus aircraft, Goodrich agreed to supply fully dressed or completed landing gear from a former Rohr engine nacelle facility in Toulouse.

In May 2001, Airbus selected Rockwell Collins to supply an avionics full duplex (AFDX) Ethernet switch for the A380, the first sole source selection for the aircraft's avionics suite. The switch provided the electronic backbone for the communications infrastructure to connect various aircraft systems, including displays, radios, and navigation sensors. The 100 megabit-per-second Ethernet network was designed to be a thousand times faster than the ARINC 429

avionics databus used in other Airbus designs. The broadband design, which was selected over a competing offer from Thales Avionics, was based on a limited 10 megabit-per-second system used on the 767-400ER, but was much larger and had enormous capacity for growth.

Thales soon rebounded with its selection by Airbus to provide the integrated modular avionics

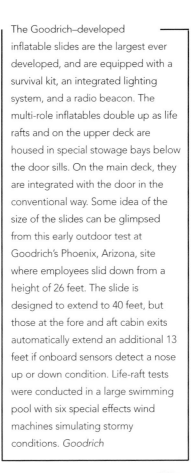

A peep inside the hidden area below the flight deck floor and above the nose gear bay inside the section 11/12 front fuselage. The radome is directly behind the box-like structure in the center of the frame, which is actually a part of the bulkhead separating the pressurized interior from the unpressurized nose gear bay. The area directly above the box is the floor of the mezzanine level flight deck. The area where the photo was taken from is used for the main avionics bay, while a secondary upper avionics bay is located in the crown of the fuselage aft of the crew rest area behind the flight deck. *Mark Wagner*

The Goodrich–developed inflatable slides are the largest ever developed, and are equipped with a survival kit, an integrated lighting system, and a radio beacon. The multi-role inflatables double up as life rafts and on the upper deck are housed in special stowage bays below the door sills. On the main deck, they are integrated with the door in the conventional way. Some idea of the size of the slides can be glimpsed from this early outdoor test at Goodrich's Phoenix, Arizona, site where employees slid down from a height of 26 feet. The slide is designed to extend to 40 feet, but those at the fore and aft cabin exits automatically extend an additional 13 feet if onboard sensors detect a nose up or down condition. Life-raft tests were conducted in a large swimming pool with six special effects wind machines simulating stormy conditions. *Goodrich*

A newly arrived Pratt & Whitney Canada PW980 auxiliary power unit (APU) sits on a raised platform awaiting installation into one of the test aircraft, MSN007, the tail section and APU exhaust of which is visible in the upper left. The engine provides bleed air for main engine starting, as well as for air conditioning, and can itself be started on the ground by either a dedicated battery or from a ground power unit. In flight, the same battery is used to start the APU or, alternatively, the aircraft's AC electrical system. The engine, designed jointly with Hamilton Sundstrand in San Diego, provides shaft power for two 120 kVA generators. *Mark Wagner*

The Honeywell flight management system, with direct links to the system most recently upgraded on the A330 and A340, is a key feature of the cockpit. Systems are checked out in the Aircraft Zero (also known as "iron bird") cockpit simulator, one of three used to help both with initial design and preparation for flight testing. For the ground tests, the simulator was fully integrated with a complete set of flight control, hydraulic, and electrical systems that were fully compliant with the test configuration planned for MSN001. *Mark Wagner*

(IMA). Teamed with Diehl Avionik Systeme of Germany, Thales offered a systems architecture in which avionics functions were distributed among generic computing modules slotted into cabinets placed throughout the aircraft. The modules were to be linked via Ethernet. To ensure safety and redundancy, other suppliers were to develop the software for avionics functions ranging from display processing to communications routing to utilities management. Thales, however, was to bid for several software packages, including the set for flight management.

July 2001 saw Goodrich awarded the contract to supply up to 18 evacuation slides per aircraft (see Chapter 13), while New York–based Parker Aerospace's Electronic Systems Division was picked to provide the fuel measurement and management systems. The system would measure fuel quantity in the massive tanks held within the wings, fuselage, and horizontal stabilizer, while the management system, controlled by the IMA suite, was designed to monitor the distribution of fuel while commanding pumps and valves to transfer fuel, handle refueling, and control center of gravity.

Another big-ticket item decided in 2001 included the air generation system, the biggest environmental control system ever built for a commercial aircraft. Awarded to Hamilton Sundstrand, the system was closely linked to the operation of the auxiliary power unit (APU), which was to be developed by sister United Technologies Company Pratt & Whitney Canada (P&WC).

Having been frustrated in its earlier attempts to lure major North American risk-sharing partners such as Northrop Grumman and Lockheed, Airbus was happy to see the U.S. and Canadian content of the A380 grow. In late 2001, a new dimension to the U.S.

growth strategy came with the announcement of plans to develop a wing design center in Wichita, Kansas.

Employing about 60 people, mainly structural and stress engineers, the center was established as a satellite office of the wing design center at Airbus U.K. in Filton, and allowed design work to continue around the clock. Although several other U.S. sites had been considered, Airbus selected Wichita because of the large number of skilled engineers already based there. Boeing, Bombardier, Cessna, and Raytheon were all local employers, but the constant ups and downs of business and general aviation, and commercial and defense markets, meant that a pool of highly trained engineers was readily available.

The U.S. content was further expanded in December with the selection of Honeywell as the supplier of the flight management system (FMS). Based on the company's Pegasus FMS, as used on the Boeing 717 and MD-11, the A380 system was expanded with new hardware for greater speed and more memory. It also featured a graphical user interface with pop-up menus and a cursor control device, rather than the more usual text-based interface. To save time, the system is list-based, allowing the crew to select from the various options rather than having to type in functions.

Although Honeywell's FMS had become standard on every new Airbus since 1984, the preceding series of nonstandard equipment selections for the A380 meant that nothing could be taken for granted. Honeywell's win over stiff competition against a combined Thales/Smiths team was therefore seen as a major victory for the aerospace company, which estimated its overall potential value at $200 million over the next 15 years.

Meanwhile, Eaton, based in Cleveland, Ohio, was selected in October 2001 to provide the high-pressure hydraulic system, and a few months later the company's aerospace unit in Michigan was chosen to provide its Aeroquip-brand Rynglok and high-pressure hoses as well. The A380 would be the first commercial aircraft to use 5,000-psi hydraulics, with only the Aerospatiale/BAE Systems Concorde coming close at about 4,500 psi.

Using the higher-pressure system produced weight savings of about 2,200 pounds, or about 30 percent less than an equivalent 3,000-psi pressure system that would have been standard on other commercial aircraft. The weight savings came mostly from reduced actuator size and smaller-diameter lines of about 1.25 inches compared to 2 inches or more for the higher pressure. Eaton expected to draw on its military experience for the A380 system, having developed the pumps and systems for aircraft such as the Lockheed Martin F-22 Raptor stealth fighter, the Bell-Boeing V-22 Osprey tilt rotor, and the F/A-18E/F Super Hornet.

Asian Ambitions

While the North American partners and supplier base were consolidating swiftly, the picture in Asia was considerably more fluid. Japan remained the number one target for Airbus, both as a source of skilled potential partners and as an untapped market, and despite almost a decade of fruitless efforts, Airbus was still determined to get Asian industry on board the A380.

The battle became particularly intense early in 2001, when Boeing upped the ante by offering Japanese industry up to 20 percent of the proposed 747X, including the entire wing. Undaunted, yet unable to dangle such a carrot, Airbus pressed on with talks with Japan's big three, Fuji (FHI), Kawasaki (KHI), and Mitsubishi Heavy Industries (MHI), as well as Japan Aircraft Manufacturing and ShinMaywa. While risk-sharing was the goal, Airbus acknowledged that simple subcontracting would help sell the A380 in prime ultra-high-capacity territory.

Internationally the risk-and-revenue program was filling up, but it continued to fall short of the 40

Some idea of the structural scale of the A380 can be glimpsed in this impressive view of the newly completed fuselage center section 15/21 of MSN006 at Saint-Nazaire, France. Measuring just over 28 feet tall and 23 feet, 5 inches wide at its widest point, the lower part of the section is also configured with support struts for the belly fairing that is attached during final assembly in Toulouse.
Mark Wagner

The gracefully sculpted wing root fairing is seen to good effect in this close-up of MSN001. Note the ram air intakes at bottom left that supply the air generation system (AGS) buried in the root area in front of the wing box. The AGS is designed to provide a fresh air flow per passenger of 0.66 pound per minute for an all-economy layout, and 0.55 pound per minute for a high-density layout. *Mark Wagner*

An inboard view of the Australian-made wingtip device that stands out 119 feet away from the side of the fuselage. The winglet looks deceptively small when viewed from the cabin, but its true size is more apparent when considering the wingtip chord is over 13 feet! The winglet takes aerodynamic loads during roll maneuvers, but is not considered a minimum equipment list (MEL) item, meaning the aircraft can be dispatched with or without them in place. *Mark Wagner*

percent of the $10.7 billion launch budget. Risk-sharing partners outside the main partners included Saab, with up to 5 percent; Hurel Dubois, with up to 2 percent; as well as AIDC (of Taiwan), Belairbus, Eurocopter, Finavitec, GKN Aerospace, Latecoere, and Stork. Italy's Finmeccanica-Alenia was also set to join (through Alenia Aerospazio) as a 4 percent risk-sharing partner with fuselage work, while Aermacchi would also become involved by the end of 2001 in the design and production of carbon-fiber nacelle parts.

Although Airbus could not quite match the Boeing wing offer, it discussed a substantial work package worth about 10 percent, including wing spoilers and ribs, cargo doors, and panels. The Airbus argument was that it—not Boeing—was the commercial powerhouse of the future, and that forging new links with Europe would provide an opening for greater quantities of commercial aviation business in the twenty-first century.

The Japanese manufacturers were in a tough position. Boeing raised concerns that its old industrial partners could risk infringing agreements with them should they invest in the A380. Furthermore, Boeing was busy pushing its recently revealed Sonic Cruiser concept, and had expressed confidence that Japanese industry would feature prominently in its development. Airbus gave FHI, KHI, and MHI until June to decide on whether or not to become risk-sharing partners, though by the end of the month it had already become clear that it was not going to happen.

After reports in the *Japan Industrial Journal* pointed to "doubts over the project's viability," it came as no surprise when FHI, KHI, and MHI reaffirmed loyalty to Boeing and rejected the full risk-sharing offer from Airbus. From here on out, Airbus' focus widened to attract second- and third-tier Japanese suppliers, which quickly began to join forces with Airbus. JAMCO, developer of the "no-slam can" (non-slamming toilet lid) for the 777 and a traditional Airbus fin part producer, was named as supplier of the upper-deck-floor carbon crossbeams, as well as stiffeners and stringers for the fin center box at its Mitaki site in Tokyo.

Others included Toray and Toho Tenax, which were signed up to supply intermediate carbon-fiber filaments for several airframe structures, while Sumitomo Metal Industries was contracted to supply titanium sheets. Some involvement from the heavies then followed when FHI, MHI, and Japan Aircraft Manufacturing all became involved as simple subcontractors. FHI was contracted to provide leading and trailing edges for the vertical stabilizer, plus the fin tip and aerodynamic fairings. The parts would be produced at FHI's Utsunomiya site. MHI, working through EADS subsidiary Eurocopter, was meanwhile contracted to supply forward and aft lower cargo doors at its factory at Oye in Nagoya. Japan Aircraft Manufacturing signed up to produce horizontal stabilizer tips at its Yokohama factory.

Later in 2002, new deals were also struck with a further group of Japanese companies, taking the island nation's potential total revenue in the A380 to well over $1.75 billion in the years to come, said Airbus. The new deals included Kobe–based ShinMaywa Industries, which was signed up for the very large main wing root fillet fairing, and the Yokohama Rubber Company, which was contracted to make composite water and waste tanks at its Hiratsuka factory in Kanagawa. Nikkiso was also signed up to provide composite cascades for the thrust reversers, which were to be fabricated at its Shizuoka plant in Haibara.

Over the following years, the potential Japanese revenue share increased to over $3 billion, according to Airbus, which later awarded a second contract to ShinMaywa for composite wing ramp surfaces. It also signed a deal with Mitsubishi Rayon for advanced composites for various A380 parts.

Australian, Korean, and Chinese manufacturers also became involved, with Korean Aerospace Industries (KAI) becoming the first Asian-based risk-and-revenue-sharing partner with a 1 1/2 percent share. Its initial contract covered the supply of 21-by-10-foot aluminum lower outer wing skin panels to be made at its Changwon factory. Australia's Hawker de Havilland company was selected to build the large A380 wingtip fences and was already a manufacturer of similar devices for the A330/A340. Ironically, Hawker de Havilland was also owned by Boeing, making it the first time the U.S. company had directly contributed to an Airbus program. (Not counting, of course, the heavily modified Boeing Super Guppy transports that had formed the backbone of the Airbus transport system since the 1970s—see Chapter 8).

China's AVIC I was later added to the subcontractor list with a deal to make the upper and lateral panels of the A380 nose landing gear bay. The work was subcontracted via the French company Latecoere, and represented the first direct involvement by a Chinese manufacturer in the A380. It seemed that the world itself was now involved in assembling the planet's largest airliner.

The nose landing gear retracts forward and is fitted with a single-stage oleo-pneumatic shock absorber. The unit is just over 16 feet tall and is steered using power from the "green" hydraulic system. The rear axle of the body landing gear unit, which also can be steered, is powered by the "yellow" hydraulic system. A ladder into the nose gear bay provides access for maintenance of the nose radar.
Mark Wagner

Airbus really owes its success to the air transport system that brought finished subassemblies, wings, and tails from the partner factories across Europe to the Toulouse final assembly line. The b[...]
Felix Kracht, the system's backbone was a fleet of bizarre-looking Super Guppy transports. Originally developed in the United States to transport sections of space rockets for NASA, the heavily [...]
transporting sections of A300Bs and later A310s. After buying the two original Super Guppies, Airbus contracted with UTA at Le Bourget in Paris for two additional conversions. One conversion, [...]
operation at Manchester International Airport in the United Kingdom. The Guppy could carry up to 170,000-pound loads in its cavernous hold, which measured 25 feet, 6 inches tall at its highest [...]
Guppies and expected to be operating it in regular service again by 2006. *Mark Wagner*

8

Land of the Giants

Developing and designing the world's largest airliner was equaled only by the massive challenges of where and how to build it. The chosen assembly site would become home to one of the greatest engineering accomplishments of the century and a towering symbol of European industrial success. Try as it might to keep the selection process from becoming mired in politics, everyone within Airbus recognized the task would not be easy.

Once more it was J,rgen Thomas who was at the forefront of the tough decision-making process when the study to find an assembly site was launched in mid-1996. The sheer scale of the A3XX meant that this was a selection process like no other. Given that the horizontal tailplane was roughly equal in size to the wing of the A310, and that the double-deck fuselage sections and the individual wings were each over 100 feet long, it was immediately obvious that the existing airborne transport system would not do.

With a land and sea transport network in the frame for the first time, the Airbus study looked at both inland and coastal locations. "We have to consider the relative advantages of transporting smaller components by aircraft to a potential inshore site, against the ability to carry complete subassemblies by ship to a coastal location," Thomas said in *Flight International* in late 1996.

Since its first aircraft was assembled in the 1970s, Airbus had relied on its unique air transport system to bring together subassemblies from all around Europe. The first-generation Super Guppy fleet was gradually being phased out in favor of the faster jet-powered "Beluga" Airbus Super Transports derived from the A300-600 airliner. But even though the planned A3XX subassemblies far exceeded the capacity of the larger

Beluga, the air link supporters were not about to give up without a struggle.

The A340 was then the largest Airbus in production, so it naturally became the focus for a piggyback wing-delivery vehicle. To support the wing, which at that stage was expected to weigh about 77,000 pounds as a monolithic unit from BAe, the derivative would be modified with a support platform to minimize changes to the upper fuselage. The wing center section would have been supported by a single frame attached to the fuselage sides, while the wing tip—which would be at the front of the aircraft—would have been attached to a smaller coupling. The main center frame would have been stressed by a triangular-shaped truss mounted inside the fuselage.

Wind tunnel tests in 1999 of the ungainly looking arrangement proved that the combination could cruise at up to Mach 0.6, cutting transport time to about four hours, versus an estimated week by sea. The tests also showed better than expected stability, despite the potential effects of the huge wing on top. As a result, Airbus believed that the only major aerodynamic modification would be a taller A330-200 fin.

Another option was to build the wings in two main sections, with the outboard being made from composites. This would have enabled the Beluga to carry the sections, with only a minor upper lobe extension required for the larger inner-wing root section.

Aerospatiale, which made no secret of its desires to have the A3XX built in Toulouse, also proposed a solution to the problem of how to transport the fuselage sections using the Beluga. Instead of assembling it from giant, truncated sections, Aerospatiale suggested dividing the fuselage lengthwise into top and bottom sections. The move, it argued, would also allow more careful matching of the completed subassemblies before the final fuselage join.

Other advantages of the air transport system over the land/sea alternative included the obvious time savings, as well as the reduced vulnerability of the supply system to industrial problems such as strike action by truck drivers or dock workers.

With so many potential options worth studying, it was little wonder that uncertainty raged for years over the site of the final assembly line that would be the last stop in either a light- or a heavy-assembly process. The light method, modeled on the traditional Airbus system of bolting together virtually complete subassemblies on the line, was obviously a problem because of the size of the assemblies, as already discussed. The heavy system, on the other hand, would require the establishment of a Boeing-like system that

threatened to disrupt the anticipated work-share arrangements of the A3XX partners.

By late 1997, the finalists had been boiled down to six potential locations, with one in Spain, two in France, and up to three in Germany. The Spanish contender was Seville—home to the assembly lines of CASA aircraft such as the 212 utility transport. Seville, considered a light site, did not make the cut, losing out to the more experienced commercial lines in more northern regions. Later, however, Seville would be awarded the valuable prize of the final assembly site of the European military airlifter, the A400M, which made it the third-largest European assembly line for Airbus after Toulouse and Hamburg.

It was between Toulouse and Hamburg that the true battle would rage, with somewhat of an unexpected twist in the tale. In the meantime, other "light" sites remained briefly in the chase. They were Saint-Nazaire on the Brest peninsula of western France and two sites in Germany: Rostock, close to the shores of the Baltic Sea by Germany's northern coast, and a remote site farther to the east by Peenemunde, on the island of Usedom. Both areas had been in the former East Germany and were undeveloped with open land and a relatively low-cost workforce. Peenemunde also had a large Luftwaffe-era airfield, having been built originally to help service and defend the adjacent World War II German rocket research site.

The choice of sites, even with Germany, was a political hot potato, particularly as DASA Airbus'

prime bid for its Hamburg Finkenwerder site had sparked an environmental controversy. To accommodate the A3XX, the Hamburg site would require a massive expansion and, after several alternatives had been examined, included leveling an old submarine factory to the east of the site. But the only realistic option was filling in part of the Muhlenberger Loch, a wetland area by the Elbe River and also Europe's largest freshwater tidal mudflat.

The Social Democrat party and, to the surprise of many, the Green Party, had supported the choice, despite the fact that the loch was home to a rare species of wildfowl. This was largely because developers were planning to reclaim only a fifth of the water and were creating a new habitat for the ducks that was twice the size of the area being filled just a few yards away. The head of the Christian Democrat party, Ole von Beust, voiced his support for the Rostock option,

Built in China, the *Ville de Bordeaux* roll-on, roll-off sea-going vessel is now the backbone of the A380 logistics chain. Visiting five ports in four countries every rotation, the ship carries fuselage, wing, and tail sections to Bordeaux from where they begin the final part of the journey across France to Toulouse. Pictured at Saint-Nazaire, the ship's massive 72-foot-wide by 46-foot-deep stern door (the largest ever built for such a vessel) is shown open to permit the loading of fuselage sections for onward carriage to Bordeaux.
Mark Wagner

long held ambitions to break the British wing monopoly that had existed since Hawker Siddeley's initial contract to make the A300 wing. DASA had recently fought hard for responsibility for the future large aircraft (later A400M) wing, resulting in a serious disagreement between the United Kingdom and German camps in 1995. DASA had signaled its intent to make a bid to lead development of a next-generation wing for the A3XX.

To help back DASA's bid, the then-Bonn–based West German government allocated DM 600 million (U.S. $327 million) for an A3XX-focused research project in 1996 under a four-year program, about half of which was for advanced wing work. To counter this, British Aerospace, along with Shorts, Dowty Aerospace, and Rolls-Royce, among others, requested £230 million (U.S. $380 million) to help support an equivalent wing, engine, and landing gear R&D effort.

Known as the integrated powered wing program, it was one of several R&D efforts the Society of British Aerospace Companies (SBAC) supported that lobbied the U.K. government on behalf of the disparate manufacturing group. In some ways, the omens for help were better than in the past, particularly when the U.K. government had dragged its feet on funding for such recent programs as the A340-500/600. The critical importance of the A3XX was much more widely recognized at high government levels throughout the continent, and the European Commission had earmarked aerospace for key action as part of its newly

stating Hamburg's site limitations and the expansive possibilities of the windswept north German plain.

While the debate raged over the final assembly site, another erupted over where the enormous wings would be built. Although wing building was traditionally the United Kingdom's specialty, Germany had

The biggest wing ever designed and built for a commercial aircraft hangs poised at Broughton for transport to France. At peak production, 1,200 people work to assemble and equip the wings, each of which weighs up to 33 tons.
Mark Wagner

ratified Fifth Framework €16.3 billion (U.S. $18.9 billion) research-and-development initiative.

Although a massive amount collectively, the European Union still urged its members to step up their support from an average of 1.9 to 2.5 percent of gross domestic product, reminding them that the United States outspent Europe in aerospace research and technology development by a factor of four. In the Fourth Framework, which was by now coming toward its scheduled closure at the end of 1998, aerospace research projects had attracted more than €400 million (U.S. $465 million) out of a total of €13.2 billion (U.S. $15.3 billion).

By mid-1999, the parts of the complex assembly jigsaw were starting to fall into place. Wing work was, to the United Kingdom's relief, allocated to British Aerospace in Broughton near Chester, but the fuselage detail remained undecided. DASA, which made the forward and aft fuselage sections of the A330/A340, argued more strongly than ever for Hamburg. Gerhard Puttfarcken, DASA Airbus vice president of product management for the A3XX, said that the piggyback A340 was essentially a waste of money, as it was geared simply toward transporting wings to Toulouse.

Instead, DASA supported a ship-borne system that would support existing centers of excellence, and suggested a single roll-on, roll-off ship that would make a weekly round-trip voyage among Aerospatiale's Saint-Nazaire factory, Chester in the United Kingdom, and Hamburg, delivering the subassemblies to support a rate of four aircraft per month. To support its bid, DASA would construct a 345-acre factory on the site of land reclaimed from the filled-in lake.

Aerospatiale countered with a proposal to help set up a huge aeronautical "park" in Toulouse and to use the Beluga to transport the top and bottom halves of the double-deck fuselage sections. To simplify mating, these would be assembled as full-length sections and joined to create the entire fuselage. The wings, Aerospatiale argued, would be carried atop the modified A340 one at a time, requiring two rotations a week.

Unique Solutions

So what should Airbus do? Looking at the lowest cost option in 2000, it finally opted for an unexpected compromise that put A3XX assembly in Toulouse but used Hamburg's Ro-Ro sea transport scheme as the transportation method. Furthermore, to satisfy German demands for a key role in final production and to relieve some pressure on Toulouse, Hamburg

Wings are transported individually on a 96-wheel trailer from the Broughton factory to the River Dee for the short journey downstream to the port of Mostyn on the north Wales coast. Ship sets are collected together for transport to Bordeaux on the Ro-Ro vessel. Note the protective coverings on the leading and trailing edges of this wing as it is prepared for loading on a Dee Dee River Craft barge. *Airbus*

Finkenwerder was allocated the task of completing furnishing, painting, and cabin production test flights. In a further twist, the split also gave Hamburg responsibility for completing aircraft destined for European and Middle Eastern customers, while Toulouse would handle the rest of the world.

The complex production and subassembly transportation system was a fantastic logistical and industrial feat of planning, with parts due to pour into Europe from all over the world. Once inside Europe's bounds, the real magic began with a carefully choreographed ballet of ships, barges, trucks, and aircraft bringing together the assemblies in Toulouse using the Airbus multi-modal transport system (MMTS).

With the start of parts manufacturing, the dance began all over Europe at roughly the same time, but the MMTS ballet commences when these parts are assembled into larger sections. The forward and aft fuselage sections are completed in Finkenwerder, where Airbus Germany had built a 300-acre plant expansion, including four hangars of 10,800 square feet each. The site also includes a cabin furnishing hall and fuselage production lines, housed in the major component assembly (MCA) hall, as well as two paint shops.

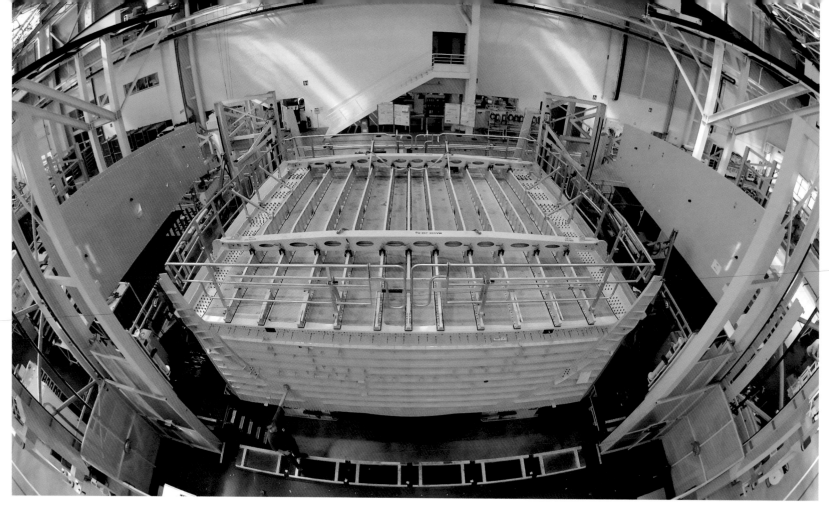

Some idea of the scale of the A380 can be gathered by this view of a completed center wing box. The complex CFRP-and-metal structure contains a host of technological innovations, including the Alcoa-developed extended performance lockbolt with a titanium collar to help join composite and aluminum parts. Alcoa, which supplies about 1 million fasteners for every A380, also supplies forgings; extrusions; sheet, plate, and castings for the aircraft's wing and fuselage skins; stringers; frames; spars; gear ribs; engine and pylon support; seat tracks; and floor beams. In 2004, Airbus spent $6.9 billion with U.S. suppliers, supporting more than 140,000 U.S. jobs. *Mark Wagner*

Once assembled with pre-installed electrical, hydraulic, and pneumatic system cables, hoses, and wires, the two sections are prepared for shipping. The subassemblies include large sections made at Nordenham and consist of an 82-foot-long aft section (combining the Airbus German-built aft fuselage with the Airbus Spanish-built rear fuselage) and the 46-foot-long forward fuselage barrel. These are loaded onto a specially built 5,200-ton Ro-Ro vessel 505 feet long and almost 80 feet broad in the beam. Although the vessel was critical to the A3XX effort, Airbus did not plan to get into the shipping business and chartered it from FRET/Cetam, a subsidiary of Louis Dreyfus Armateurs of France and Leif Hoegh of Norway. This company, in turn, commissioned the building of the ship by Jinling Shipyard in Nanjing, China, in March 2002.

The ship's keel was laid in February 2003, and it was launched from the banks of the mighty Yangtze River just six months later. Christened the *Ville de Bordeaux*, she featured the largest watertight stern door (72 by 46 feet) ever built on such a vessel and had 72,334 square feet of space on the cargo deck. After fitting out, the vessel sailed from Nanjing to Yizheng

farther down river in April 2004 before departing China via Shanghai for its long delivery voyage to Europe.

From Hamburg, the *Ville*'s first voyage on its regular bus route took it across the North Sea and through the English Channel, around Land's End and into the Irish Sea. Rounding Carmel Head just off the island of Angelsea, it nosed its way into the Dee Estuary, docking at the North Wales coastal port of Mostyn. Here it took on the Airbus U.K.-built wing set, each wing measuring 147.5 feet in length and weighing 72,700 pounds.

The wings were made at an all-new west factory in Broughton, United Kingdom, across the runway from where Hawker Siddeley once assembled the highly successful HS 125 (later BAe 125) business jet, and from where all the other Airbus wings are made. As with these structures, the skins, spars, ribs, and stringers were to be brought to the site from Filton, Bristol.

The wings for the wide-body aircraft such as the A300 and the A330/A340 are assembled at Broughton before being flown by Beluga to the Airbus Germany site in Bremen for fitting with control surfaces and on to delivery to Toulouse. The narrow body wings for the A320 family are fully equipped at Broughton before delivery to either Hamburg (A318, A319, A321) or Toulouse (A320).

In the case of the A380, about 25 percent of the wings are fabricated at Broughton; the remainder come from Filton and subcontract suppliers such as Saab, which was to produce the mid and outer fixed leading edges. Each set would comprise 32,000 parts, with additional assemblies from Belairbus (leading edge), Airbus Germany (flaps), and Airbus France (spoilers/ailerons) being added in Toulouse. The west factory houses the main assembly jigs, where the A380 wing components and subassemblies are loaded and assembled into a wing box, and a wing-equipping area, where fuel, pneumatic, and hydraulic systems and wiring are installed and tested. The wings are then loaded one by one on a Dee Dee River Craft barge for the short journey down the river to Mostyn for transfer to the Ro-Ro vessel.

From here the ship retraces its course as far as Land's End, before heading due south across the channel past Brest and the jutting Finisterre peninsula to Saint-Nazaire, where one forward fuselage is offloaded so a locally built nose section can be attached. Here Airbus France also incorporates the all-composite cen-

A380 cockpit sections come together on the line at Méaulte. The cockpit window frames are made from machined AL 7040 aluminum alloy, while the tall windshield fairing above the flight deck is made of chemically milled aluminum skins clad over machined ribs directly over the windshield, and machined frames above and aft the window line. The upper stringers in the top of the crown are extruded. Just below the windows is a specially strengthened bird impact shield. *Mark Wagner*

Boxes of belly fairing parts arrive at the final assembly line by road from Spain. The massive fairing is built up from sandwich panels made up of a Nomex honeycomb core and a hybrid carbon-glass-fiber epoxy skin. A substructure made from aluminum alloy sheet metal will support these panels in place. The stringers and frame roots on the lower part of the fairing are made from corrosion-resistant titanium. *Mark Wagner*

91

Towering almost 48 feet above the fuselage and an almost unbelievable 79 feet, 8 inches above the ground, the vertical tail follows in the Airbus tradition of being constructed of composite with a solid-laminate CFRP fin box cured in an autoclave, or giant oven, at 180 degrees Celcius. The vertical stabilizer covers an area of 1,316 square feet and is swept back at an angle of 40 degrees as measured at the 25 ercent chord point. The Spanish-made rudder is taken from Puerto Real to Stade in Germany, where it is attached to the fin. The complete structure is then flown to Toulouse in the Beluga. *Mark Wagner*

The road transport convoy winds its way through the French countryside toward Toulouse. Tractor one, with the left wing set, usually leads the convoy, with tractor two following immediately behind with the right wing. Next, tractor three pulls a trailer with the massive V-shaped horizontal stabilizer; tractors four, five, and six make up the remainder of the convoy with the three fuselage sections. Some 26 gendarmes help escort the convoy, at least six of whom ride motorcycles in front of the tractors. *Airbus*

The passage under the historic Pont de Pierre bridge at Bordeaux is a matter of good timing for the crews of the river barges taking the A380 subassemblies up the River Garonne from the port. Although the barges have special ballast systems to lower their profile, the crews usually aim for a three-hour low-tide window to ensure good clearance. *Airbus*

ter wing box of the A380 built in Nantes and transported to Saint-Nazaire by road, as well as incorporating the center part of the Spanish-made belly fairing in the center fuselage. The two parts of the nose section of the fuselage, which by now also contain the cockpit, are subassembled at Méaulte, nearby in France, and sent by road to Saint-Nazaire. A completed forward/nose assembly is then loaded for the short voyage along the coast and past La Rochelle, down the curving estuary of the Gironde to the Pauillac terminal in Bordeaux harbor.

Having discharged its cargo, the *Ville de Bordeaux* then sets sail on a fourth trip, which takes it west and south beyond Cape Finisterre along the Portuguese coast and past Lisbon and Cape St. Vincent to the Spanish port of Cádiz. Here it takes aboard another immense belly fairing and the Puerto Real–built 89-foot-span horizontal tailplane, the latter weighing 7 tons. Airbus Spain's Getafe factory near Madrid produces the aft fuselage, main gear doors, dorsal fin, composite rudder, and belly fairing. Although the latter goes south to join the ship at Cádiz because of its size, the aft fuselage section is flown by Beluga to Finkenwerder for attachment to the German-built rear fuselage. Meanwhile, the rudder is taken by road from Puerto Real to Stade in Germany for attachment

to the fin while the ship turns around at Cádiz and heads back to Bordeaux with its new load.

At the Pauillac terminal, the massive subassemblies, still in their palletized holding fixtures, are off-loaded directly onto a floating transfer station. Brought to Bordeaux from Gdansk, Poland, the station is almost 495 feet long, 115 feet wide, 25 feet high, and weighs 3,500 tons. The unusual flat-topped station transfers the loads to a pair of specially designed barges that are fitted with a variable ballast system. This allows them to float lower in the water when necessary and enables them to pass under all the bridges on the River Garonne, even in flood stages. Made by the Netherlands barge builder De Hoop in 2003, the vessels are operated for Airbus by Socatra.

The vessels travel for 12 hours along the Garonne as far as Langon, the farthest practical point up river for large-scale barge movements, and discharge their cargo at a specially built wet lock in Langon harbor. The parts are then marshaled together in a remarkable convoy that could have jumped straight from the pages of Jonathan Swift's *Gulliver's Travels* as it winds through the pastures, geese farms, and vineyards of the Landes and Gers regions toward Toulouse.

Organized by the freight company Capelle, the convoy consists of specially developed trailers from Nicolas/Scheuerle pulled by 600-horsepower Mercedes-built tractor units. The trailers have multi-steering capability, height adjustment, leveling compensation, and even their own guidance system. Including gendarmes (French police) on motorcycles, escort and support vehicles, and the tractor-trailers, the convoy consists of 43 vehicles, 26 gendarmes, 8 pathfinders, and 29 drivers and operators.

First comes the port wing, followed by the starboard wing, the horizontal tailplane, the aft fuselage, the forward fuselage, and finally the center fuselage. Avoiding the fast Route Nationale A62 between Bordeaux and Toulouse, the convoy snakes along back roads through the countryside by night to avoid disrupting traffic. Traveling through small towns and villages such as Bazas, Captieux, Maillas, Lapeyrade, Gabarret, Cazaubon, Eauze, Vic-Fezensac, Gimont, L'Isle-Jourdain, and the larger market town of Auch, the journey takes three nights, with up to four en route parking areas available to the convoy before finally arriving at the Aeroconstellation complex. Now the hard work can really begin!

Being readied for the flight test in the equipping and test station 30/31 area after being shunted in from the final assembly station 41/40, work proceeds around the clock on the first flying aircraft

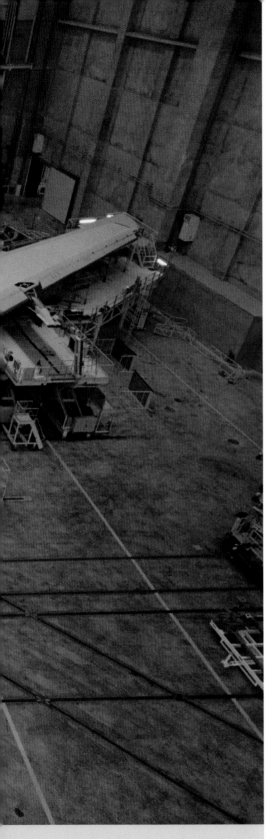

9
Cutting Metal

All across Europe through the winter of 2001–2002, companies prepared to start manufacturing the first components of the A380. The first official metal-cutting ceremony was in Nantes, France, on January 23, 2002, where work began on the A380 wing root fairing nose as well as the center wing box.

The start of machining began with work on a piece of structure called the "cross." Together with the "tee," the cross was at the very heart of the A380 where the center wing box joined the upper part of the center section. The massive center wing box measured 23 by 20 by 7 feet, but was about 2,200 pounds lighter than a similar-sized metal part thanks to the extensive use of composites, which made up more than 50 percent of the structure. Carbon fiber was used for forward and aft spars, as well as for upper and lower panels. Assembly of these parts also began on January 23.

In March 2002, the Bremen site also began A380 production with two formed sheet aluminum parts, which would form part of the aft fuselage. Airbus Germany's Varel site began work the following month on the first aluminum frame assembly for the rear fuselage, while production also began at the other German facilities in Nordenham and Stade. In the United Kingdom, the first metal cutting for parts of the wing took place in April at Filton.

As work was beginning on the various parts of the new airliner, many of the facilities also saw massive building construction projects starting up for the A380 program. By far the largest of these was in Toulouse itself, where a huge plant covering more than 123 acres was underway just a short drive from the Blagnac Airport. Built as part of the prestigious

new Aeroconstellation Park, the site consisted of the static test building and the final assembly hall, which covered an area equivalent to 20 soccer fields. Arranged in a series of adjoining hangars with gently curved roofs, the building was 1,600 feet long, 820 feet wide, and 150 feet tall. It was one of the biggest buildings in the world, incorporating more than 32,000 tons of steel, or the equivalent of four Eiffel Towers.

Preparation for the site, which was to be named Jean-Luc Lagardére after the cochairman of EADS at the time of the A380 launch and one of its fiercest supporters, also started in April 2002. The final assembly hall roof was raised into place in sections in mid-February 2003, and was all but complete by the end of the year. As well as providing sufficient space for final assembly of up to six superjumbos simultaneously, the hall also accommodated 365,900 square feet of office space.

Close by, construction work had also been underway since January 2002 on a static test building, modeled on the same lines as the individual hangars making up the massive final assembly line building. Covering 129,160 square feet, this building became officially operational by mid-2003 and was ready to

house the static airframe that would be a vital part of the A380 certification effort.

A new office on the Toulouse St. Martin site carried out the design work and the release of drawings to production. There, more than 1,000 people worked on eight floors over a total area of almost 182,990 square feet. The process of drawing release, under which final engineering designs were passed on to production, had started as a trickle at the start of 2002 and passed the 120,000 mark by the end of the year. It soon zoomed to about the 330,000 mark, or about 95 percent by late 2003. At the program's peak, more than 5,000 engineers worked on the A380 (including the -800F), and by early 2002, the figure was already about 4,700 engineers. The peak, at about 5,200, was expected to be reached in early 2003, with a gradual fallback toward 3,000 engineers as the project moved into flight test and full production.

Near the St. Martin site, another new building with 204,500 square feet of space was erected to house three A380 flight-deck simulators and the "iron bird," an unusual test rig that replicated all the major systems of the aircraft. The iron bird was used for systems integration and verification and, together with one of the simulators, was so complete that it was dubbed Aircraft Zero. Tests with the iron bird began in December 2003, when the combined Aircraft Zero cockpit and systems rig (flight controls, hydraulic, and electrical) was the same as that in the MSN001.

Pneumatic and cabin systems, including water and waste, were tested in special rigs developed in Hamburg, home of Cabin Zero. The new building also housed a cabin technology device, which was mounted on a moveable platform to simulate the effect of sloping positions, standing impacts, and even runway rambling. It also housed a virtual-reality lab to assess other cabin redesign alternatives, a full cabin integration rig that enabled the full linking of the AFDX (avionics full duplex) Ethernet network with the cabin systems, and the IMA modules and their applications. The site also helped evaluate relatively late interior design changes, which saw new manufacturers such as California–based C&D Aerospace become involved in supplying the crew rest module and other parts of the A380 interior. In-flight entertainment (IFE) tests were performed separately by Thales in a 555-seat lab in Irvine, California.

Adjacent to the Cabin Zero area, work was well under way to complete the new 346-acre site on reclaimed land in Hamburg. Protected from possible coastal and river flooding by a dike, the site housed the A380 major component assembly hall (MCA Hall) work that began in March 2002. The building was almost 750 feet long, 393 feet wide, and 75 feet tall, and was made to house the forward and aft fuselage sections, and to "stuff" the subassemblies with all the necessary systems.

Also being built on the site were a cabin furnishing hall, a delivery center for the formal handover of aircraft to European and Middle Eastern customers, two paint shops, a preflight hangar, and an engine run-up site.

By now, work on the Broughton wing site in the United Kingdom was complete, with a new 226,050-square foot building to make stringers for bottom wing skin panels being completed in mid-2002. Extensions to other existing skin mill and creep forming buildings was completed by the end of the year and well before the official opening of the £350 million (U.S. $578 million) U.K. site by Prime Minister Tony Blair. At over 1,310 feet in length and more than 656 feet tall, the new west factory covered an area equal to 12 soccer fields, and, at its peak, would employ up to 1,200 people.

Farther south in Filton, construction of the world's largest landing gear test rig was completed across the runway from the famous "Brab" hangar, the historic home of the U.K. Concorde assembly line, as well as the production line for aircraft such as the Bristol Britannia and, of course, the Brabazon. By early 2003, work was also under way at the site on a new integrated machining facility for wing ribs. Drop tests in the Filton facility began in July 2004, while extension and retraction tests were completed by the end of November. To make the rig extra realistic, it was integrated with a real aircraft electrical network and associated avionics.

Even farther south in Spain at Getafe and Puerto Real, new assembly facilities for the horizontal tailplane and the enormous 105-foot-long belly fairing were completed. The facilities covered 204,500 and 161,460 square feet, respectively. In Illescas, just outside Madrid, a plant extension housed new fiber placement machines for tape lay-up of parts for several carbon-fiber fuselage sections.

The first center wing box for flight test aircraft MSN001, weighing in at 25,550 pounds fully equipped, was delivered by barge from Nantes to the

Saint-Nazaire plant by the mouth of the Loire River in August 2003. Within a few weeks, the forward fuselage (section 12) was ready for fitting out at Mèaulte and was joined by the cockpit (section 11). The first landing gear bay was also delivered from Mèaulte to Saint-Nazaire, where the job of fitting together the first forward fuselage subassembly was about to begin with the combination of the German-built forward fuselage (section 13) and the French-built cockpit.

Meanwhile, the first 75-foot-long center fuselage sections (15/21) had been completed and moved out of their jig at Saint-Nazaire in preparation for the installation of the Spanish-built belly fairing. The rest of the center fuselage was also coming together with the integration of the structurally complex Mèaulte-built main landing gear bays and the Nantes-made center wing box.

The section also included the Sogerma-produced floor grid and the forward lower shell and part

Although this might not look much like an A380, so many of the aircraft's systems are in this maze of tangled steel and wiring that the test rig is known as Aircraft Zero. Located at Toulouse, the test rig, which is also known more familiarly as the iron bird, is used to replicate the A380's major flight control, hydraulic, and electrical systems. The actual control surfaces, including the rudder seen rising up inside its support scaffold toward the rear of the site, are connected to the systems to evaluate their readiness. In the latter stages of development, a cockpit simulator was also connected to the rig (see Chapter 7).
Mark Wagner

Supplying the water needs and handling the waste of more than 500 passengers on a long-range flight are daunting technical challenges. They required a special water/waste test rig all their own set up at Hamburg where pneumatic and cabin systems were developed. The rig simulates the aircraft's water system, which features four main potable water distribution lines, two per deck, and baseline storage in six tanks with a volume of 1,700 liters. Waste water is drained down ducts with a slope of at least 2 degrees relative to the aircraft's X and Y axes. Four vacuum waste pipes are located in the aircraft, two per deck, and feed into four waste collection tanks with a capacity of 2,300 liters.
Airbus

of the upper shell, both made by Alenia at its Turin and Naples sites in Nola and Casoria, Italy. It also included the 39-foot-long central lower fuselage shell, which was supplied by SABCA of Belgium. This formed a load-bearing support between the wings and rear fuselage and also channeled several hydraulic and electrical systems; it was covered in the aft part by double-curved, stretched, and chemically milled skins. The forward skin was mechanically machined from a single piece of aluminum plate.

The first unpressurized two-part aft fuselage (section 19), consisting of the largely composite struc-

ture supporting the vertical and horizontal stabilizers and the aftermost tail cone housing the auxiliary power unit, was also transported by Beluga to Finkenwerder for attachment to the aft fuselage (section 18). In November 2003, the first rear fuselage aluminum ring frame, 24.5 feet in diameter, was delivered from Varel to Hamburg. The ring connected the rear fuselage to the composite rear pressure bulkhead and formed the interface between the rear fuselage section and the Spanish-made aft fuselage. Airbus Germany's Donauworth site also took delivery that month of the first Mitsubishi-built cargo door, which was shipped from Nagoya.

November 2003 also saw Malaysian supplier Composites Technology Resource Malaysia (CTRM) hand over the first set of composite leading-edge wing components from Malacca to Airbus U.K., where the first wing set had been removed from its jigs at Broughton. By January 2004, the wing was being fitted out with hydraulic and fuel-system wiring prior to delivery to Toulouse in April. The 66,000-pound structure measured 119 feet root to tip in length, was 36 feet wide and almost 10 feet deep at the root where the wing met the body. Meanwhile in the United

States, Los Angeles–based Hitco Carbon Composites marked the official handover of the first ship set of vertical tail carbon-fiber–reinforced plastic truss structures to Airbus Germany.

In Germany the vertical tail had been completed for the first static test airframe, dubbed the *essais statiques* (ES) in the Airbus assembly firing order. Assembly of the first two flying aircraft, MSN001 and MSN004, was also under way by January 2004, with the tail for the fatigue test airframe, the *essais fatigue* (EF), started in March. Parts for the MSN001 and ES airframes entered final assembly at Toulouse at virtually the same time, although the static test airframe would be the first to be completed by July 2004. Full-scale fatigue tests were to be undertaken in Dresden, Germany, by IABG (Industrieanlagen-Betriebsgesellschaft), the engineering company that had previously tested other Airbus types, most recently the A340-600.

Testing, Testing

By May 2004, the first static airframe was coming together in Toulouse in a new process in which it was assembled at a single station, rather than moving it through several assembly stations in the factory. Under the new process, the fuselage sections, wings, and tail were brought to one station before the complete air-

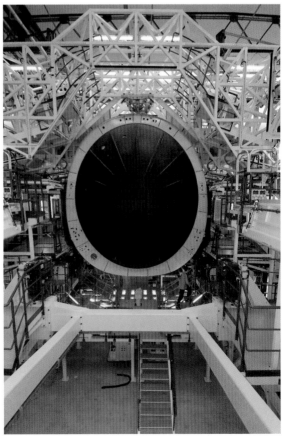

The first vertical tail fin arrives at Toulouse from Germany in the Beluga. The complete vertical tail is virtually the only large part of the A380 that is transportable in the traditional Airbus way, comfortably fitting into the Beluga's huge 123-foot-long main cargo compartment. *Airbus*

The piece de resistance of the Toulouse final assembly line is the 41/40 single station used to join the massive parts of the fuselage and wings together. The laser-aided spatial positioning (LASP) system uses high-tech optics to align the jigs and subassemblies and works out the exact dimensions of each section. The system then confers with the computer-aided three-dimensional design system, which calculates the exact positioning of the piece using its data-based knowledge about the section's structural characteristics, dimensions, and average tolerances. All this is achieved within a matter of hours and to within accuracies of a few millimeters. *Mark Wagner*

frame was moved on its own wheels to one of three sites for completion and systems tests. In a full production aircraft, this would entail fitting of the engines, auxiliary power unit, fixed leading edges, and landing gear doors. Once completed, the aircraft was then to be taken to one of 10 outside positions for engine and APU runs, pressurization and fuel system tests, and weather radar evaluation and other tests.

On May 7, 2004, French Prime Minister Jean-Pierre Raffarin inaugurated the $425 million (at that time Ä360 million) Jean-Luc LagardÈre Production Complex, and on May 27, the static test airframe was quietly rolled off the production line and into the adjacent test hangar. Although it was the world's first real look at the A380, the ES was the poor ugly duckling without most of its empennage, engines, radome, or even paint. Naked in its simple primer, the aircraft was quickly hidden from view while work went on to complete assembly of MSN001, the real star of the show to come in January 2005.

The static test building was a worthy engineering feat in its own right, with a vaulted ceiling height of just over 95 feet under the hook cranes in the roof and standing on concrete reinforced with about 1,000 tons of steel. Mounted inside the test rig, which itself weighed 1,000 tons, the airframe was supported on 306 jacks and connected to 8,000 gauges. For the actual tests, several structural parts were replaced with dummy parts, including the horizontal and vertical tails, the entire tail cone, the slat and flap tracks, the

engines and pylons, and the landing gear. The tests would be concluded dramatically with the gradual bending of the wings to their maximum elastic limit. Engineers predicted these would eventually break with explosive force when they were bent upward at the tip by about 33 feet!

The static and fatigue tests formed the top of what Airbus called a test pyramid. Below the major tests were big-ticket component tests on the empennage, sub-components, details, elements, and down to small parts or "coupons." Other component tests included a piece of fuselage made up of GLARE skin, as well as aluminum stringers and frames, and a curved pressurized panel that had been laser welded. Goodrich and Dowty also conducted separate landing gear static and drop tests, while a further series of tests also evaluated the resistance of the cockpit windows to bird impacts.

Subassemblies for MSN001 came together on the first assembly station (41/40) in Toulouse on the same day the static airframe rolled out. By July 7, the aircraft

was structurally complete and able to move on its own wheels to the next completion station (31/30). Work on MSN002 began a few days later, just as the five major subassemblies of the next aircraft (MSN004) arrived by convoy. Further back up the line, parts of aircraft MSN007 and MSN003 were being built in Saint-Nazaire, while assembly of components for MSN015 had already begun at Nantes. In the United

Kingdom, work was under way on wings for five aircraft, while in Germany the final touches were being put on the aft fuselage of MSN007, and the fin of MSN004 was virtually complete. Construction of tailplanes for six aircraft was under way in Puerto Real, Spain.

The magic moment of "power on," the moment when the aircraft officially begins to come alive, was on July 30, 2004, when the electrical generation and distribution system were powered up on MSN001 for the first time. Six weeks later, sections of the A380 were on the move again, when the EF fatigue specimen

(the third airframe built) began its long journey upstream along the River Elbe to the test site at Dresden. Assembly of the structure was completed by the end of February 2005, and by September of that year it would begin to run through the first of up to 47,500 simulated flights to test the fatigue life of the airframe. Testing would last nearly 26 months.

To help put together the EF aircraft, the Toulouse-based assembly team briefly moved to Dresden to set up the test airframe, which, they hoped, would amass 5,000 hours of time by the scheduled certification of the A380 in 2006. IABG's contract called for the completion of up to 900 "flights" per week, with the rig operating 24 hours per day. Weighing almost 1,000 tons, the test rig consisted of 190 hydraulic jacks; 7,200 strain gauges; and hundreds of deflection, pressure, and temperature sensors.

Although targeted at 47,500 cycles by 2008, this was actually calculated to be equal to 60,000 flights, because it was to be fatigue loaded to a slightly higher factor of 1.1 per hour. The structure was due to be inspected every 4,000 hours for any signs of fatigue damage, with each flight consisting of a full fuselage pressurization cycle and an average of 480 load cases covering the stresses and strains likely to be encountered during a typical flight, including everything from taxi, takeoff, climb, maneuver, and descent to landing and braking.

Assembly of the fourth flight test A380, MSN007, began in Toulouse on November 18, after the return of the construction team from Dresden. Preflight test work meanwhile was well under way on MSN001, which had spent over two months at station 30 having checks performed on the trimming functionality of its large horizontal stabilizer, as well as other tests on the flight controls, slats and flaps, undercarriage extension and retraction, brakes and steering, and bleed air system. MSN001 (and MSN004) were also fitted with a representative mini-cabin section in a small area of the upper fuselage, complete with sidewall and ceiling panels, overhead storage bins, and even a galley and lavatory.

Following completion of these initial fittings, MSN001 was moved outside for fuel and cabin pressurization tests at station 18 before being trundled into the paint hangar for finishing in its new blue Airbus corporate livery. Only MSN001 and MSN004 were to be painted at Toulouse, with all others flying to Hamburg for completion at the two new specially built paint hangars at Finkenwerder.

Following the "reveal" (see Chapter 15), preflight work continued at station 22 to swap out non-flight-

rated systems and equipment that were installed during the initial build process, in addition to upgrading or changing items as a result of lessons learned during the first ground-test phase. Final checks and flight preparation then were undertaken at station 17, where items such as the deployment of the ram-air turbine, thrust reversers, and operation of the radios and oxygen system were carefully checked.

With all the boxes ticked, MSN001 was cleared to carry out taxi tests and low-speed acceleration and stop checks. After all these years, it was difficult for the gathered Airbus employees to believe that the A380 was finally moving under its own power. After several more days of brake and system checks, the superjumbo was cleared to be taxied to the end of Blagnac's 11,480-foot runway 32L for high-speed runs and a full stop. The urge to take the aircraft on its first flight was almost irresistible, but it would have to wait.

A magic moment for Airbus, the customer airlines, and thousands of suppliers on October 11, 2004, when for the first time three aircraft were in the final assembly line at station 30/31. They included MSN001 in the background, MSN002 in the middle distance, and MSN004 in the foreground. MSN001 would conduct the first flight on April 27, 2005, while the second aircraft into the air was the medium-duty flight test and cabin system evaluation airframe, MSN002. The third aircraft, MSN004, was due to follow, with the fourth test aircraft, MSN007, right after that. *Airbus*

The gulling effect of the A380 wing is pronounced in this head-on view. Designed to maximize ground clearance for the high-bypass-ratio engines in the event of an awkward "rolling" landing w
pylons made largely from titanium with a thermoplastic-carbon and aluminum secondary structure. The nacelle cowl is made from an epoxy CFRP outer barrel, with similar material used for the f

10
Absolute Power

When the throttles are advanced for takeoff, the A380's four engines pump out an incredible 280,000 pounds of thrust, more than any commercial jetliner in history. With heavier future models, such as the freighter, total power will increase to more than 320,000 pounds of thrust. At their ultimate potential, the A380 engines have been designed to collectively generate up to 336,000 pounds of thrust, compared with the 260,000 pounds of a current 747!

The engines that powered the A380 for its maiden flight in 2005 are different from those Airbus first envisaged 15 years earlier. The early studies revolved around the use of A330-sized engines for improved cost, schedule, and development. But as the size of the UHCA family grew beyond 600 to 800 passengers to include a 1,050-seater, the studies had to include six-engine variants to stay within the thrust capabilities of this engine class.

General Electric, Pratt & Whitney, and Rolls-Royce were also, at the time, each in the thick of developing new engines for the Boeing 777. These would prove to be the largest commercial jet engines yet built, and because they were designed for a twin-engine aircraft, they were too big to be used on the multiple-engine UHCA and VLCT designs floating around in the early 1990s.

The key difference between a twin-engine and a four-engine aircraft is that the former are takeoff-thrust limited, while the four-engine designs are climb-thrust limited. The reasoning behind this is simply that a twin must have sufficient power to continue to take off on one engine alone, should it suffer an engine failure on the runway. Individual engine power requirements are therefore not as high in four-engine aircraft, which have more

Darkening the sky overhead with its sheer size, the enormous, one-and-only Antonov An-225 "Mriya" (Dream) is still the largest jet aircraft in the world. With a wingspan of 290 feet, the fly-by-wire six-engined design inspired early UHCA concepts, most of which focused on the possibilities of 700 to 800 seats with a similar number of powerplants. Grounded for many years, the An-225 returned to flight in 2001 as a special freighter and continues in operation today. With a wingspan of just over 261 feet, the A380 is the second largest aircraft in terms of span, but obviously reigns supreme as the biggest passenger aircraft ever built. For comparison, other giant jets include the An-124 Ruslan, with a 240-foot span; the Lockheed Martin C-5 Galaxy, with a 222-foot, 8-inch span; and the Boeing 747-400 at 213 feet. *Mark Wagner*

thrust available from the remaining three engines should they suffer a powerplant failure on takeoff.

In particular, the focus for a four-or-more-engine superjumbo design was on top-of-climb thrust. The ratio of takeoff thrust to top-of-climb thrust in a big twin and a conceptual UHCA was dramatic. The initial 777s, for example, required about 84,000 pounds of thrust per engine for takeoff, and about 16,900 pounds at the top of climb. By contrast, the new, large airliner would require about 75,000 pounds of thrust for takeoff and close to 20,000 pounds for top of climb.

None of the engine makers deluded themselves when it came to development costs for the next new generation, however. Stan Todd, the erstwhile director of Trent engines at Rolls-Royce, said in 1994 that, "aircraft makers are diligently studying various concepts for VLAs [very large aircraft], which, if committed, would be the biggest investment decision the civil aircraft industry has yet taken."

Given the sheer scale of the projected designs, it quickly became obvious to all players that a mega-twin was out of the running. "A twin-engined VLA is an option in theory, but the required engine size is at least twice the thrust of any engine so far developed, but the investment would be huge and the market base would appear to be too limited to support that level of investment in the foreseeable future," said Todd.

With their 116-inch-diameter fans, the Engine Alliance GP7200 and Rolls-Royce Trent 900 engines are the largest ever to power an Airbus airliner. Total potential thrust output from the initial engines is in the 280,000- to 300,000-pound range, more than any previous jetliner. *Mark Wagner*

GE argued at the time that there were advantages in going to the other extreme with as many as six engines in a configuration similar to the Antonov An-225, the largest jet-powered aircraft ever made. "The advantage with having more than four engines is with redundancy. A six-engine aircraft down to five engines is not going to have a great problem in completing its mission," said a GE spokesperson. Aside from stating the obvious, however, GE also acknowledged that the "likelihood is that the VLA will have four powerplants."

Then there was the crucial issue of noise, which from the outset was aimed to be equal to or less than the noise generated by the 747, and certainly well below the limits agreed by the International Civil Aviation Organization (ICAO) under Annex 16, Chapter 3 (or equivalent U.S. FAR 36, Stage 3) with environmentally perceived noise decibel (EPNdB) targets of about 100 for flyover, 98 for sideline, and about 100 for approach. To achieve these noise-level targets, the engine makers were concerned that modifying existing engines could incur too great a performance or cost penalty, and increasingly the focus was on all-new designs.

Rolls-Royce looked at three concepts for its large aircraft study, all developed from the baseline three-shaft Trent 800 then in test for the 777. The first, dubbed the Trent 895X-119, was an enhanced design for increased top-of-climb performance. The second, the T895X-142, had a considerably larger fan diame-

The initial Trent 900 was based on a scaled-down version of the core of the Trent 800, one of which is pictured here. As the noise requirement of the A3XX changed dramatically in late 1999, Rolls-Royce and the Engine Alliance were forced into late revisions of their respective designs. Both increased fan diameter by up to 6 inches to 116 inches, making the Trent 900 the largest engine ever built by Rolls-Royce in terms of fan size. To perfect its design, Rolls-Royce turned to an advanced fan design originally developed for the Trent 8104, a 100,000-pound-plus study engine originally aimed at the ultra-long-range 777-200LRX and -300ERX, but which never entered production.
Mark Wagner

ter, while the third, the T895X-164, was a more radical departure with a variable-pitch fan and fan-drive gear system.

Although all three had similar overall pressure ratios, temperature limits, and noise performance, they differed significantly in terms of weight, size, specific fuel consumption, and bypass ratio (BPR). The BPR for the standard-configuration engine was 6.5, the larger-fan version's BPR was 10, and the variable-pitch fan had a whopping BPR of 13.5.

By early 1996, both the emergence of the A3XX and the Boeing 747-500X/600X projects had given the engine makers firmer requirements to aim at. Boeing aimed for a service entry target of 2000 to beat Airbus to market, and Rolls-Royce soon adopted a low-risk approach to satisfy the U.S. manufacturer's fast-track goal. In July 1996, Rolls-Royce signed an agreement with Boeing to offer a relatively simple derivative of the Trent 800 dubbed the Trent 900.

Trent Tradition

The heart of the Trent 900 was a scaled-down Trent 800 core attached to a 110-inch-diameter fan, with a slimmer, lighter nacelle. By reducing the core size and yet retaining a large fan, Rolls-Royce was able to increase BPR from about 6.5 on the Trent 800 to nearer 8.5, or fairly close to the target BPR of the T895X-142 study engine. For the 747X, it was to be offered at thrust levels from 78,000 to 80,000 pounds, putting it slightly higher than the thrust needs of the A3XX, which were then envisaged at between 69,600 and 75,000 pounds.

Internally, the Trent 900 was configured with a scaled core similar in size to what would soon become the Trent 500, the new engine for the A340-500/600. In particular, it consisted of scaled-down Trent 895 intermediate-pressure (IP) and high-pressure (HP) compressors, a new five-stage low-pressure (LP) turbine, and reduced-loading IP and HP turbines. Headed by Charles Cuddington, the Trent 900 project quickly assumed a greater role as Airbus sought a choice of engine for the fledgling A3XX. The engine project was launched formally at that year's Farnborough Air Show, while talks with Airbus assumed a new level of intensity after signing the agreement with Boeing. Finally, in November 1996, Rolls-Royce and Airbus signed a memorandum of understanding to provide an engine in the 72,000- to 79,000-pound thrust range for the A3XX.

Then, when it seemed as if all systems were go, Boeing suddenly dropped its 747-500X/600X plans only a month later, throwing doubt on the engine maker's plans. Without the urgency of the 747 derivative, which called for a fast-paced 33-month development effort, the wind suddenly was taken from Rolls-Royce's sails. Instead of aiming for certification in December 1999, the engine maker now viewed a considerably more distant notional in-service date of 2003 at the earliest.

The delay was enough to see risk-sharing partners such as Kawasaki Heavy Industries (KHI) opt out of the original program, which ticked along at a relatively slow pace through 1997 and into 1998. But with the rising tempo of the A3XX effort, a new team of risk- and revenue-sharing partners began to join the program. Over the next five years, the team grew to include FiatAvio, Goodrich, Hamilton Sundstrand, Honeywell, Marubeni, and Volvo. Samsung Techwin of Korea and IHI of Japan also participated as program associates. In June 2003, KHI also rejoined the Trent 900 program as an associate with responsibility for the IP compressor casing.

The design continued to be refined against the original specifications, but in late 1999, the emergence of tough new quota count (QC) noise laws planned for

The pronounced scimitar-shaped edge to the elegantly curved and twisted Trent 900 fan blades are shown to good effect in this close-up of an early production engine pictured at Rolls-Royce's Derby site in early 2005. As with earlier designs, the swept titanium blades of the Trent 900 are hollow and made using a modernized version of the superplastic diffusion bonding process that Rolls-Royce pioneered for the first wide-chord blades used on the RB.211-535E4 engine. Further back inside, the engine sports several features derived from the Trent 500 used on the A340-500/600, including scaled versions of the eight-stage intermediate-pressure (IP) compressor, six-stage high-pressure (HP) compressor, single-stage IP turbine, and five-stage LP turbine.
Mark Wagner

The remarkable twist of the Trent 900 wide-chord blades is clearly shown in this view through a fan set being prepared for delivery for one of the flight test aircraft early in 2005. At full power, the 24 fan blades suck in more than a ton and a half of air every second, while the total power produced by the four engines at takeoff is roughly equal to the power produced by 3,500 family automobiles. *Mark Wagner*

— The extraordinary-looking, multicolored Trent 900 fan is specially painted to enable recording and monitoring equipment to pick out the behavior of specific blades during blade-off tests in which a blade is deliberately detached from the hub in the center of the engine at full power. The test is crucial to successful certification, and with the Trent 900 having an all-new large fan design, Rolls-Royce took great care in the buildup to these tests. Here preparations are being made for a rig test to prove the trailing edge blade integrity in preparation for future blade-off testing. The engine subsequently passed a blade-off rig test in August 2003 and the full-engine blade-off test, in which the multimillion-dollar test engine 90007 was effectively ruined, the following July. *Rolls-Royce*

— Engine tests also included evaluations of performance with the new Hurel-Hispano–built nacelle, one of which was the cross wind ground test pictured here using engine 90003. Hurel-Hispano provided the new nose and fan cowls, thrust reverser, and exhaust nozzle, and delivered the first units to Rolls-Royce in July 2003. *Rolls-Royce*

— Another crucial requirement for all modern jet engines is the ability to withstand the impact and ingestion of birds. Under a more recent certification requirement, the engine makers had to show the engine could continue operating after taking a hit from a 5.5 pound "flocking" bird, typically a goose. Test engine 90005, which had earlier been used for blade flutter, nacelle, and thrust reverser tests, is prepared to undergo the bird ingestion test. Note the high-speed camera, illuminated inlet, and numbered fan blades. *Rolls-Royce*

London Heathrow Airport posed a potential new threat to the final configuration. It soon became obvious that under the new QC rules, the A380 operators would be penalized heavily at Heathrow if the airframe and engine design remained as it was.

As a direct result, several late design changes were made (see Chapter 6), details of which were announced at an Airbus customer symposium held in January 2000. For the engine, it meant some major—and extremely last-minute—revisions, the biggest of which was the increase in fan diameter from 110 to 116 inches, making the Trent 900 the biggest engine (in terms of fan size) ever built by Rolls-Royce. "We had to change the LP system within only a few months, but our design people had lots of options under their belt," said Rolls-Royce Marketing Vice President Robert Nuttall.

The larger fan was based on the Trent 8104 configuration, a three-dimensionally designed, forward-swept fan that was originally aimed at the 777-200X/300X but which ended up as a technology demonstrator. The eight-stage IP compressor was also Trent 8104-based, and both the LP and IP turbines were scaled up, the former now about the same size as the fan on the RB211-535 engine on the 757. The fan case also had to grow to accommodate the larger bypass requirements.

For the first time on a Rolls-Royce Trent, the HP turbine was designed to counter-rotate, and in tests it had shown a 2 percent efficiency gain as it optimized the flow entering the IP turbine, requiring fewer nozzle-guide vanes. The vanes that remained were also subject to less stress and were therefore smaller and lighter by design.

At the end of 2000, Rolls-Royce won the first engine competition when SIA selected it to power its 10 firm and 15 option A3XXs. The deal was a crucial strategic victory over the General Electric and Pratt & Whitney Engine Alliance, and gave Rolls-Royce pole position in the race to gain the lead in the superjumbo power market. By the time the first Trent 900 fired up at Rolls-Royce's Derby test site on March 18, 2003, the engine had clinched a 57 percent share of the firm orders, with subsequent wins at Qantas, Virgin Atlantic, Lufthansa, and International Lease Finance Company.

By April 2, the test engine had achieved its certification thrust level of 81,000 pounds. On April 9, the engine reached 88,000 pounds thrust, which was "not for bravado," said Nuttall. "It was literally to push the engine for data on extreme operating conditions," acknowledging that the initial Trent 970 version

Dwarfing the A340-300's standard CFM International CFM56 engine, the powerful Trent 900 hangs on the inboard position of the Airbus flying testbed at Toulouse. Rated initially at 70,000 pounds thrust, but having topped 93,000 pounds in tests, it easily became the largest and most powerful engine ever to fly on an Airbus aircraft when the test effort started with a 3-hour, 41-minute flight on May 17, 2004. As well as some basic engine performance work, the flights were mostly aimed at investigating aircraft-related systems such as the 5,000-psi hydraulic system and variable-frequency electrical generator system. Although the formal flight test effort concluded in 2004 after 60 hours, some tests continued into 2005 to support the A380 flight test program.
Mark Wagner

would be rated at 70,000 pounds thrust for entry into service. The critical blade containment test was passed successfully in August 2003 and was "even more impressive because it involved the largest fan ever used in a Rolls-Royce engine," said Ian Kinnear, director of Airbus programs.

By the end of 2003, five test engines were running in the certification effort and were showing performance that was "on spec for weight and fuel consumption and emissions targets. It's now officially the world's lowest emission large fan engine," said Cuddington, who by now was Rolls-Royce managing director for airlines. The only significant glitch cropped up that year during an endurance test when, with the engine passing the 115-hour mark, a nozzle guide vane came loose and hit two LP turbine blades. With the help of the IPT design team in Spain, the seal segment and retaining ring were strengthened to prevent a repeat of the failure.

Flight tests were undertaken on the well-used A340-300 previously used as an all-purpose testbed for several other tests ranging from flight control system experiments to other engine tests, including the Trent 500. The first flight was made on May 17, 2004, and lasted 3 hours, 40 minutes. With 60 hours of flight tests under its belt, Rolls-Royce completed a final full-scale blade-off test in July and, at the end of October 2004, achieved its European Aviation Safety Agency (EASA) airworthiness certification. According to Airbus, the engines also performed flawlessly on the big day for the A380 when they powered the prototype into the air for the first time on April 27, 2005, truly marking one of the crowning achievements in the growing civil success story for the British engine maker.

The Grand Alliance

In May 1996, the aerospace world was stunned when GE Aircraft Engines and Pratt & Whitney jointly announced an agreement to develop a new jet engine for the Boeing 747-500X/600X aircraft. The joint engine development program covered the 72,000- to 84,000-pound thrust range and was agreed between the two archrivals after a standard prelaunch sparring session earlier in the year. Boeing, said the joint statement, "urged the two companies to explore the joint program."

No wonder. GE had been struggling to improve the operability of the GE90, which had become an expensive development program that was well over budget. Boeing too was financially tied and was by now in the thick of certification efforts on three separate and expensive flight-test programs for the GE-, P&W-, and Rolls-Royce–powered 777, and had itself been attempting to explore the joint VLCT initiative with the Airbus partners. Boeing figured the

A crucial sales and logistics consideration was designing the engine to be able to fit into the main deck cargo hold of a Boeing 747 freighter. With a fan diameter of 116 inches, the manufacturers realized it would be a tight squeeze so they did everything to try and minimize the overall outer geometry of the engine, particularly the fan case. Based on earlier proof-of-concept rig tests on a Trent 500–sized fan assembly and containment system, Rolls-Royce introduced a revised, smaller design than the standard aluminum/Kevlar containment package. The new system was also lighter, which proved vital in making it easier to transport on a 747. Loading demonstrations were successfully conducted on a 747-400F (which has a slightly smaller door than the -200F) at Stansted in the United Kingdom on February 28, 2005.
Rolls-Royce

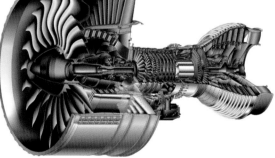

market for the new 747 was likely to be too small to cope with the complications and costs of another three-way engine fight, and the cut-and-thrust had already begun with GE offering a CF6-80X, P&W offering a modular powerplant based on the PW4000, and Rolls-Royce offering either a modified Trent 700 or a de-rated Trent 800.

It was with these thoughts in mind that a couple of GE and P&W executives began to casually chat about the situation over drinks one day at the Singapore Air Show in February 1996. They both agreed that to meet Boeing's tight timescale, GE and P&W needed new engine designs in the same thrust range and time period. Given that it would be a relatively limited production run, the real economic answer, they argued, was to team together. GE had the new GE90 core that P&W admired, while P&W had new fan technology, enabling a neat technical fit. The idea was proposed to the chief executives of the two companies, Gene Murphy at GE and Carl Krapek at P&W, and following their joint approval the venture was launched pending the approval of the European Union which, because of potential antitrust issues, was required to bless the marriage.

This joint venture, called simply the GE P&W Engine Alliance, was unveiled at the 1996 Farnborough Air Show that September. Engines were to be assembled at a line at P&W's East Hartford, Connecticut, site using elements from both companies. GE was to supply the GE90-derived high-pressure-core technology with P&W's low-pressure technology based on the PW4000 series. Launch engine was to be the GP7176 for the 747-X, while a second engine, the GP7200, was aimed at the A3XX.

Plans called for a 36-month certification effort to run from the start of 1997 to meet a certification target of December 1999. But it was the Engine Alliance's turn to be stunned when, less than four months after the company was founded, the Boeing 747-500X/600X plan was abandoned. Although a proposed GP7100 version was later aimed at the more modest 747-400X and -400ERX studies, the new focus was now firmly on the Airbus superjumbo project.

To the surprise of some, including possibly those within the alliance, Pratt & Whitney still maintained a dialogue with Airbus over the separate choice of a new PW4000 derivative dubbed the PW4500. By mid-1997, however, Airbus made it clear that only two engines would be offered, and J‚rgen Thomas acknowledged that "we are evaluating both offers from the United States," while still considering the Rolls-Royce Trent 900.

But the rift soon disappeared, and on December 18, 1997, the Engine Alliance began installation studies with Airbus aimed at finalizing a firm engine configuration by mid-1998. By now the core consisted of a nine-stage HP compressor (instead of the original 10-stage unit) and a two-stage HP turbine "that still looks like the GE90's," said the newly appointed president, Bruce Hughes. "Pratt & Whitney will provide the fan section based on the hollow titanium blades of the PW4084 and low-pressure system based on the PW4168. The one thing we're looking for is reduction in shop costs."

Despite the Airbus-imposed delay on the A3XX in early 1998, the Alliance's mood remained upbeat. "All in all the delay is a good thing. It gives us more time to add new things," said Hughes. By mid-1999, the Alliance said the final configuration of the engine was scheduled to be frozen in May 2001, setting the clock running on a certification target in November 2003. Within months, however, the engine was in consideration for two twin applications—a proposed-growth A330-300 and Boeing's 767-400ERX, and the Alliance opted to raise the tempo of the development program, accelerating the planned milestones by nine months.

Soon this timetable was once more in flux, following the decision to redesign the engine to bring it in line with QC/2 requirements. As with the Trent 900, the Alliance designers were forced to increase fan diameter to 116 inches, raising the fan bypass ratio from 8:1 to 9:1. The changes added stages to the LP compressor and turbine, as well as noise-reduction features, including swept, hollow wide-chord fan blades, contoured exit-guide vanes and re-optimized blade and vane counts in the LP compressor and turbine.

Further core tests got underway in early 2001 under the newly installed president, Lloyd Thompson, with a further revised schedule calling for the first full engine test to run in early 2004. First flight on the A380 was scheduled for January 2006.

May 2001 saw the Engine Alliance clinch its first order when Air France selected the GP7200 to power 10 firm A380s, and crowned this with a major win the following February when Emirates chose the engine to power 22 firm and 10 optioned aircraft. The deal, worth about $1.5 billion, pushed the Engine Alliance into the lead over Rolls-Royce. Further orders arrived in July 2002, when FedEx, as long expected, picked the GP7277 version to power its fleet of 10 A380-800Fs.

More re-jigging of the schedule followed in early 2003 when the Engine Alliance decided to bring forward the first planned full GP7200 engine test by two months to mid-February 2004 to give more margin for lessons learned before the expected certification in 2005. Part of the time was allotted to extra tests of the swept-blade design, which was described by P&W GP7200 Vice President Bob Saia: "The shape gives it efficiency and reduces the shock loss as the flow goes

Designed for low noise, the key features of the GP7200 include the swept-fan blades, extensive acoustic treatment in the fan case, significant axial spacing between the fan blades, and contoured fan exit guide vanes visible in this drawing of the back of the wide bypass duct. The engine also features carefully positioned blades in the LP compressor and turbine to produce an acoustic cancellation effect, as well as a chevroned core exhaust nozzle, which is not shown in this illustration. *Engine Alliance*

Carefully positioned lighting picks out perfectly the swept-fan blades as a test engineer inspects the casing around the HP compressor. The engine team elected to stay with an enlarged version of the P&W titanium-based design rather than select a composite GE90-style design when it was forced to grow the fan by 6 inches to meet more stringent QC/2 noise rules after 2000. Revenue-share partners in the program include Snecma and its Techspace Aero subsidiary as well as MTU of Germany. *Engine Alliance*

from supersonic to subsonic at the tip." The enlarged metallic shape had been selected in March 2002 over an alternative composite-blade design, which had been proposed the year earlier as part of the QC/2 redesign.

December 2003 brought the welcome news that Emirates had once again selected the GP7200 for a massive follow-on order of 23

additional A380s, for delivery from 2009 onward. The total meant that Emirates had ordered 199 engines, valued at more than $3 billion, making the GP7200 the best-selling engine on the A380 at that time.

Initial runs of the engine finally got underway at East Hartford on March 10, 2004, but unexpected surges in the cruise condition caused by compressor vane scheduling problems hampered efforts to quickly demonstrate high thrust levels. These problems were eventually ironed out, and in early April the engine reached 80,000 pounds thrust, eventually topping out at 86,500 pounds thrust in the Airbus configuration (88,000 pounds when adjusted to P&W's measuring conditions), before the first phase of the testing was completed after 45 hours.

Unexpected issues also cropped up on the second GP7200 test engine, which started running at Peebles, Ohio, in early May. After the test engine was decelerated, "we noticed a vibration shift. We shut it down and found bits of metal in the tailpipe, and then we found we had lost the outer third of one blade," said

Thompson. The trailing edges of the second-stage HP turbine were trimmed, and a longer term modification involving stiffening the blade was also devised. Better news came from the performance data, which showed an exhaust gas temperature that was 10 degrees Celsius lower than expected, as well as cruise-specific fuel consumption that was 0.5 percent better.

Flight tests began on GE's 747-100 flying testbed in bright, clear weather at Victorville, California, on December 3, 2004, roughly three months behind the original schedule. Initial work focused on engine operability, but because of the need to add modifications to the HP compressor and HP turbine, the full flight test evaluation was rescheduled for later in 2005. All testing was wrapped up in the summer of 2005, with the engine's long-awaited certification set for the third quarter. Meanwhile, the first flight of the GP7200-powered A380 was due around November 2005, the first ship set of engines having been delivered to Airbus over the previous three months.

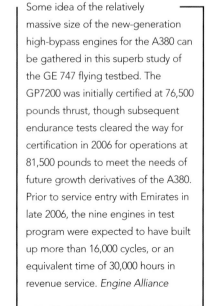

Kicking up dust and sand, the General Electric–operated Boeing 747-100 flying testbed carries the GP7200 into the air for the first time from its flight test base at Victorville, California, on December 3, 2004. Mounted in the traditional inboard position in the left wing, the flight lasted three hours and focused on assessing engine operation and on gathering propulsion system data on the nacelle and accessories. The initial test phase paved the way for a full-up flight test effort later in 2005 using a production-standard engine with several improvements added to the aerodynamics of the core. *Engine Alliance*

Some idea of the relatively massive size of the new-generation high-bypass engines for the A380 can be gathered in this superb study of the GE 747 flying testbed. The GP7200 was initially certified at 76,500 pounds thrust, though subsequent endurance tests cleared the way for certification in 2006 for operations at 81,500 pounds to meet the needs of future growth derivatives of the A380. Prior to service entry with Emirates in late 2006, the nine engines in test program were expected to have built up more than 16,000 cycles, or an equivalent time of 30,000 hours in revenue service. *Engine Alliance*

The changing contours of the A380 fuselage are subtly revealed in this foreshortened view of MSN001. The fuselage is spherical from the radome aft as far as frame 31 between the forward carg

main deck. Aft of this area, just forward of the large letter A in "Airbus," the fuselage assumes an ovoid cross section that is constant for the remainder of the fuselage. Although the overall leng

deck is actually only about 168 feet. The upper deck is 154 feet, 10 inches long. *Mark Wagner*

11
Engineering a Giant

Outwardly very different from any aircraft before it, the A380 is beneath the skin a finely balanced blend of high-tech materials, structural advances, and traditional Airbus design know-how.

Wrapped around the unique ovoid cross section, the overall aircraft shape was optimized in the presence of all other airframe components using computational fluid dynamics—a first for any Airbus. The process cut drag by 2 percent, which was particularly vital for the relatively blunt body and stubby nose section.

Aside from its sheer scale and its double-deck configuration, the structure itself is relatively traditional, but with a wealth of new materials, such as GLARE and reinforced thermoplastics. The aircraft also features carbon-fiber–reinforced plastic frames in the tail cone section and, for the first time, welded stringers in the lower fuselage.

Built to last for a design service goal of 19,000 flight cycles, 140,000 flight hours, or 25 years, whichever comes first, the A380 is more ruggedly constructed than any previous Airbus. Advanced aluminum alloys form the semi-monocoque structure of the fuselage, while the skins are chemically milled or machined to reduce the all-important weight. GLARE is used for the upper and lateral fuselage skins of the forward and aft section above the main-deck level, again mostly for weight reduction, while welded stringer panels are used in the lower fuselage sections below the main deck floor.

The panels for areas in the landing gear bays and other highly loaded sections such as the lower center fuselage are machined in tandem with integrated stringers for extra strength. The massive frames that run the length of the aircraft are also heavily loaded.

and the second passenger door on the
he aircraft is 230 feet, the cabin main length

Where stresses are particularly high—such as near cutout surrounds (around doors and hatches), the wing root area, nose and center fuselage lower shells—critical parts are machined. In less highly loaded areas, such as the upper shell, parts simply are extruded.

The nose section is another unique Airbus feature, containing a large unpressurized area in the forward lower part for the nose gear bay. The remainder of the nose fuselage, which is called section 11/12, runs aft from the radome to frame 22 and includes the flight deck, crew rest area, electronics bays, and passenger door 1. Locally welded longitudinal stringers stiffen a double-curved panel that forms the internal upper-pressure bulkhead inside and behind the nose gear bay.

Tapering aft from the circular radome, the fuselage is still spherical where it becomes section 13 at frame 22. It remains this way all the way back to frame 31 between the forward cargo bay door and door 2, where it assumes the constant ovoid cross section.

A clear depiction of the main structural elements of the A380-800 showing the forward, center, and aft fuselage sections, which are 72 feet, 75 feet, and 92 feet long, respectively. Note the relative length of the enormous belly fairing, picked out in purple. *Airbus*

A380-800 Main Structural (Parts) Components

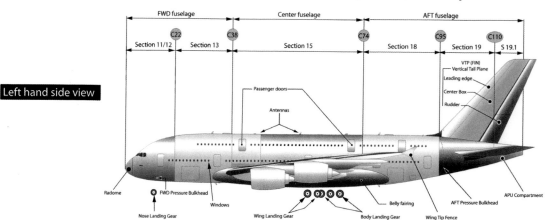

Left hand side view

FWD fuselage | Center fuselage | AFT fuselage

C22 | C38 | C74 | C95 | C110

Section 11/12 | Section 13 | Section 15 | Section 18 | Section 19 | S 19.1

VTP (FIN)
Vertical Tail Plane
Leading edge
Center Box
Rudder

Passenger doors

Antennas

Radome
FWD Pressure Bulkhead
Nose Landing Gear
Windows
Wing Landing Gear
Body Landing Gear
Belly fairing
Wing Tip Fence
AFT Pressure Bulkhead
APU Compartment

Welded stingers stiffen the skins on the lower side of this section, and GLARE strengthens the upper shell above the main deck door level. The upper-deck cross-beams are made from carbon-fiber–reinforced plastic and are connected to the frames by shear joints and supported by vertical struts, while the main deck beams are made from aluminum alloy. A floor grid sits on top of the beams and supports composite floor panels that are sealed in place for corrosion protection.

A double-width stairway, designed to be passable by two passengers with hand baggage simultaneously and located by door 1, has hand rails that enable its use for in-flight movements. An aft staircase, cunningly recessed into the curvature of the rear pressure bulkhead, is reached by door 5 on the main deck and winds up to the upper deck. The stairs are designed to be wide enough for a stretcher to be carried up or down, or for crew members with service equipment.

The middle chunk of the fuselage, section 15/21, runs from frames 38 to 74 and is the largest and most complex fuselage subassembly Airbus has ever made. The section includes doors 7 and 8 on the upper deck, and door 3 on the main deck, as well as the center wing box and belly fairing. It also includes the main

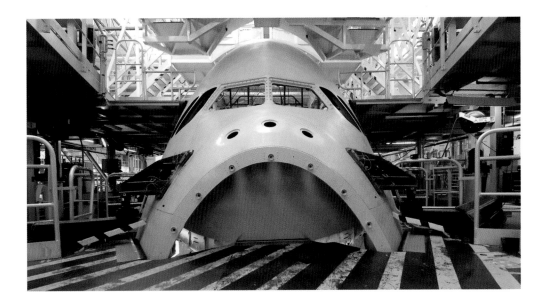

landing gear bay, which takes up the area between the rear spar of the center wing box at frames 56 and 72. The wing gears, each with a four-wheel bogie, stow into the forward area between frames 56 and 63, while the six-wheel body gears stow into the rear area between frames 63 and 72. A traverse wall separates

The unusual "vertically stacked" flight deck and nose assembly line at Méaulte reveals the equally unusual new nose concept that was adopted to meet the deep-profile requirements of the double-deck design. Note the curved bulkhead panel forming the lower section of the cockpit floor. The nose in the foreground was destined for MSN014, the first A380 for Qantas, while the nose in the background will eventually fly for Emirates. *Mark Wagner*

A rare early glimpse inside the cavernous main deck of an aircraft destined for Singapore Airlines. The width of this deck is 21 feet, 7 inches at its widest point, 18 inches larger than the 747. The upper deck is 19 feet, 5 inches wide at its widest point, a full 46 percent bigger than the relatively narrow upper deck of the famous Boeing. Note the CFRP upper deck floor beams made by JAMCO of Mitaka, Tokyo. *Mark Wagner*

The difference between the floor crossbeams on the two decks is clearly shown in the view of the cross section. Note the dark CFRP beams supporting the upper deck, while the main deck beams are made from AL-Li C460/2196 aluminum-lithium. Seat rails on both decks are made from AL 7349/7055 aluminum, while the lower skin panels are made from laser-welded panels of AL 6013 aluminum alloy. *Mark Wagner*

The double-width forward staircase is 5 feet wide, making it passable simultaneously by two passengers with luggage, and is a fixed installation located on the main deck adjacent to door 1 left and right. The stairs are designed to be used in-flight during cruise. *Airbus*

Curving into the recessed aft pressure bulkhead, the 15-step rear staircase joins both decks and provides access to the aft main cabin area that is seen mocked up as a meeting area, library, and in-flight shop in this Airbus creation. Some airlines are studying using the upper deck area at the top of the stairway for a cabin crew rest area with up to 12 bunks and a shower. *Mark Wagner*

the wing and body gear bays on each side.

The enormous belly fairing is formed from a series of panels made up of a Nomex honeycomb and hybrid epoxy skin sandwich. An aluminum substructure that supports these panels helps transfer some of the fuselage loads to the fairing by deformation between the primary structure of the fuselage and the belly fairing support structure.

The aft fuselage, section 18, runs from frames 74 to 95 and includes passenger doors 4 and 5 on the main deck and door 9 on the upper deck. The fuselage also encompasses a cargo door on the right side and a bulk cargo door on the same side farther aft between frames 87 and 89. At frame 95, the aft section is attached to the unpressurized rear fuselage, which consists of a forward unit (section 19) and a tail cone (section 19.1). A dome-shaped carbon-fiber–reinforced plastic rear-pressure bulkhead separates the tail section from the rest of the aircraft.

Although a relatively small piece of structure compared to the main fuselage, sections 19 and 19.1 are complex assemblies. The double curvature of the composite panels, which are "area-ruled" for transonic flow conditions at the root of the horizontal stabilizer, are made up by using an automated fiber-placement technique. Highly loaded frames, which support the attachment for the massive vertical tailplane, are machined from high-strength aluminum alloys, while weight-saving nonmetallic frames made from resin transfer molding make up several of the less loaded frames. A double row of six lugs and 12 shear bolts attaches the base of the vertical tail fin to the fuselage using the same design concept as the A340.

Just forward of the first set of lugs is the large frame at station 108 supporting the horizontal tailplane pivot points, while a single trim screw is positioned between frames 99 and 100. Aft of this is the tail cone—mainly consisting of carbon-fiber–reinforced plastic skins, frames, and stringers—that houses the auxiliary power unit. A titanium rear fairing encompasses the aft-facing APU exhaust, while the compartment itself is lined with firewalls made from titanium sheets.

The vertical stabilizer towers almost 48 feet high, taking the overall tail height to an incredible 79 feet, 5 inches. The stabilizer has a chord of 39 feet, 6 inches at the root, not counting the dorsal fairing, giving an aspect ratio of 1.74 and a taper ratio of 0.39. The tail is also relatively sharply swept back at 40 degrees, measured at the conventional 25 percent chord point. Overall, the vertical tail is about the same size as the A320 wing in span, and almost the same chord width as the A340-500/600.

Both the fin and rudder are of a new design that uses a single torsion box and an upper and lower rudder, the latter being just over 16 feet high. The fin box is made up of carbon-fiber–reinforced plastic with two full-span front and rear spars, web and framework ribs and fittings for rudder support made from CFRP, and

Among the sturdiest parts of the A380 are the strongly built wing and body landing gear bays located on either side of the T-shaped cargo compartment that juts forward from the aft cargo section up to the center wing box. Looking more like the inside of a battleship than the airborne "cruise liner" concept Airbus proffered, the cutouts are made from machined panels with a transverse wall separating the wing and body gear bays. Note the self-stiffened panels making up the inner and upper walls of the bays. *Mark Wagner*

The laser-welded skin of the lower fuselage section 18 is shown at Hamburg along with the white area to the right of the cargo door opening that will hold the rear section of the belly fairing attachment. This "busy" fuselage section includes door 4 of the main deck, the rear cargo compartment access door, and an entry door for the bulk cargo compartment. The two compartments are separated by a net. *Mark Wagner*

The rear unpressurized fuselage section 19 holds the attachments and reinforced substructure for the fin and horizontal tailplane. It is a cleverly constructed composite structure made from CFRP panel skins, attached to highly loaded aluminum frames, and slightly less loaded resin transfer molded frames. To make the large unit, the entire structure is turned on a mandril for optimum ply distribution. *Mark Wagner*

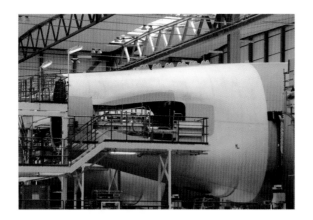

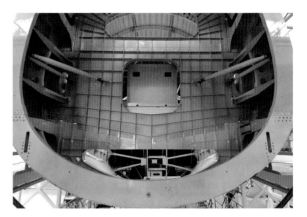

Shown here under construction in Stade, the left-hand skin panel for the CFRP–made fin box of MSN008 contains the attachment holes for the 12 double-shear lugs and bolts that will be used to attach it to the fuselage. The fin box consists of two full-span front and rear spars, web and framework ribs, and fittings to support the composite rudder. *Mark Wagner*

A view from the rear of section 19 before the tail cone (section 19.1) is attached shows the heavily reinforced structure that takes the lateral loads of the horizontal tailplane. On the other side of the transverse structure, roughly opposite where the struts are seen attached nearest to the fuselage sides, two bulky fittings provide the pivot hinge point for the huge horizontal stabilizer. The position for the single screw jack that moves the trimmable surface is visible through the small cutout at the base of the structure. *Mark Wagner*

A series of 12 aluminum forged fittings, each with holes for two shear bolt joints, are riveted to two adjacent frames and skin in the top of section 19. Note the double curvature of the skin by the space where the root of the horizontal stabilizer will go. This aerodynamic feature is "area-ruled" to accommodate for the supersonic speed of the local airflow around the stabilizer, thereby mitigating any drag rise. The concept of "Coke bottle" or area-ruled shaping was the brainchild of Richard Whitcomb, a NASA Langley engineer who won the 1954 Collier Trophy for his work. *Mark Wagner*

resin-transfer molding material with aluminum-alloy end fittings.

The horizontal stabilizer runs through section 19 and includes an integral fuel tank between ribs 8 left and right. The fuel level in the tail tank, which can take up to 23,698 liters, is adjustable in flight for trimming purposes. Overall, the baseline A380-800 fuel-tank capacity is 315,292 liters, most of which is contained in two inner tanks with more than 90,600 liters. Two other mid-tanks hold about 72,000 liters between them, with inner engine 2 and 3 feed tanks containing 28,130 liters each. The outer engine 1 and 4 feed tanks each hold 26,974 liters, while the two outer tanks each hold 9,524 liters.

The screw-driven trim system can adjust the angle of attack of the horizontal stabilizer through an angle ranging from plus 3 degrees up to minus 10.5 degrees down. As with the vertical tail, the horizontal unit is an all-new design with CFRP torsion box. The elevator is split into two about midway along the trailing edge, with each part being separately actuated. Overall, the tail span is just over 99 feet, which is 5 feet longer than one wing of the A340-500/600, or 6 feet wider than the wingspan of a 737-200!

Structurally speaking, two of the most impressive features of the A380 are the enormous 261-foot-6-inch-span wings, which cover a massive

area of 9,104 square feet—second only to the 9,741-square-foot area of the six-engined Antonov An-225. With an aspect ratio of 7.52 and a 33.5-degree sweep angle at the 25 percent chord mark, the wings have a dihedral of 5.6 degrees at the tip, which has a chord just over 13 feet.

Each wing supports two engine pylons, the wing main landing gear, three ailerons for low-speed flight, and eight spoilers for roll control, lift dumping, or gust load alleviation. The leading edge also supports two droop noses and six slat sections, while three single-slotted Fowler flap sections hang off the trailing edge. The inner flap is metallic, while the two outer flaps are made from composites, as are the spoilers and ailerons.

The primary structure is made up of a metallic outer part and a hybrid CFRP/aluminum-alloy center box consisting of front, center, and rear spars, upper and lower skin panels, and root rib. Frame fittings attach the center wing box to the upper fuselage, while the upper fuselage skin is bolted to a large structure called the upper cruciform flange. The inner part of the wing from ribs 1 to 17 has front, center, and rear aluminum-alloy spars, while outboard of this to rib 49 there is only a front and rear spar. To save weight, 23 of the 49 ribs are fully or partially made from CFRP, most of them occurring mid-span between the engines.

With a root chord of 39 feet, 6 inches and a height roughly equivalent to an A320 wing, the impressively tall tail of the A380 will be an increasingly eye-catching sight at airports around the world in the twenty-first century. The rudder is split into two for yaw control, with each part controlled by a pair of electric backup hydraulic actuators (EBHAs) from independent hydraulic and electrical systems. In normal operation, the actuators are active and driven by the flight control computers. If a hydraulic system failure occurs, the affected actuators automatically revert to electrical mode. These operate slightly slower but still provide maximum rudder deflection of plus or minus 30 degrees. *Mark Wagner*

The impressive array of flaps and spoilers and the elegant curvature of the A380's massive trailing edge are well-illustrated in this view of MSN001 coming to a halt at the end of its maiden flight. The overwing surfaces are a combined set of airbrakes, spoilers, and lift dumpers, at least six of which are visible in this shot. On the landing roll, spoilers 3 through 8 provide a maximum deflection of up to 45 degrees rising to 50 degrees for lift dumping when firmly on the ground. The metallic strip visible in the aft section of the belly fairing near door 4 is a flexible joint to allow the composite shell to flex as it absorbs the bending loads of the body. *Mark Wagner*

These bizarre-looking bulges on the pedestal between the pilots are the cursor control devices (CCDs). Unlike the regular "mouse" of a desktop PC, the trackballs have to be built into these rai operated in turbulence. Using the cursor or the keyboard mounts ahead of the CCDs, the displays effectively become interactive. With Windows-like display formats, the crew can use the CCD menus. They can even use the device to steer the aircraft by clicking on a "direct to" command that interacts with the flight management display to direct the aircraft toward a new waypoint. M

12
Systematic Approach

Beneath the skin, the A380 is packed with technical advances and innovations across a wide range of avionics, systems, and hardware—all designed to help the crew operate the world's largest jetliner as easily as if it were an A320.

Many of these advances are visible on the flight deck, which is roomier than a 747 cockpit because of its mid-level mezzanine location. Dominating the cockpit are eight Diehl Avionik Systeme–developed 7.25-inch-by-9.25-inch liquid crystal displays (LCDs) on the main panel and forward center pedestal. Unlike previous Airbus glass cockpit displays that are essentially square, the A380 LCDs are arranged in a portrait configuration to allow more data to be added to the display.

In particular, the navigation display (ND) will show a vertical, or side-view, display of the flight trajectory at all stages of flight. This extra safety feature is expected to be especially useful during descent and final approach, as it will show the actual flight path of the A380 relative to the terrain profile. Minimum safe altitude or lowest safe descent heights are also shown graphically on the vertical display.

The Honeywell-developed aircraft environment surveillance system (AESS) handles overall threat warning and awareness. The AESS also combines information about potential conflicts with other air traffic, weather hazards such as wind shear, and enhanced ground proximity and warning.

When the aircraft is on the ground, the ND will revert to a system dubbed "Taxi Driver" that puts the A380 as a symbol in the center of a screen depicting its position on a moving-map display of the airport. Outboard of the ND is the primary flight display

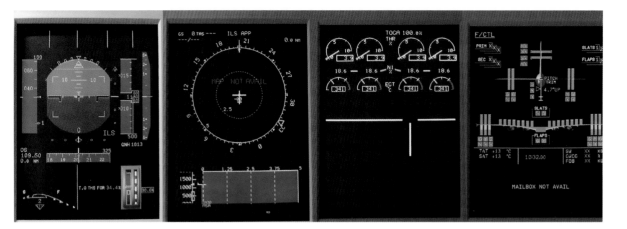

The onboard information terminal (OIT) occupies the extreme corners of the flight deck, just ahead of the side stick controllers on either side of the cockpit. Developed by Sagem, the onboard information system (OIS) hosts a massive digital memory and effectively replaces all the paper charts and weather maps that crews once carted on board by the bagfull. It also manages maintenance records and passenger records and controls the flow of data to and from the aircraft via either a gatelink when on the ground or via satellite communications once en route. The crew interface with the OIS through a keyboard and pointer found under the foldaway tray in front of the pilots. *Mark Wagner*

New display features will help enhance safety on the A380, as seen in this montage of screen displays. The navigation display on the far left, for example, shows a vertical situation display at the base of the screen that clearly shows the aircraft's altitude profile relative to the ground. The system displays the projected flight path in profile and immediately will warn the crew graphically and aurally if the planned flight path is putting the aircraft in danger. Overall, the aircraft is better protected than any previous generation of airliner thanks to the myriad safety systems grouped together as part of the Honeywell aircraft environment surveillance system (AESS). Integrating the traffic alert and collision avoidance (TCAS), enhanced ground proximity warning (EGPWS), and weather radar, the AESS uses data from each to help refine the overall surveillance picture. For example, AESS uses EGPWS data to alter the tilt angle of the weather radar antenna to optimize the scan along the intended flight path without picking up too much clutter from the terrain. *Mark Wagner*

Pilots familiar with the other Airbus family members will feel at home on the flight deck of the A380, though will welcome the improvements, including a total of eight 6-inch-by-8-inch large-format liquid crystal displays (LCDs). These include two primary flight displays (PFDs), two navigation displays (NDs), two multifunction displays (MFDs), an engine/warning display, and a single systems display. Not shown here in this development simulator (Aircraft 1) are the thales-developed LCD digital heads-up displays that will be available as a factory option. *Mark Wagner*

(PFD), which, at its base, will display configuration data critical to the flight phase or airspeed, such as airbrake or flap selection.

In the central position between the PFD/ND screens is the Airbus-standard electronic centralized aircraft monitor (ECAM), which combines engine/warning and systems display functions on two screens. Two multifunction displays (MFDs) sit at either side of the lower ECAM display on the central pedestal between the pilots. On either side of the power levers are the pilot's keyboard cursor control units (KCCU), which are linked to the MFDs and provide the crew with their main interface with the flight management system (FMS). This is a next-gen-

eration graphics-based system developed by Honeywell based on the Pegasus FMS already used in the A320 and A340.

Built into the KCCU is a cursor-control trackball and a selector that allows crews to point and click their way through menus on the MFD or to make flight plan alterations by selecting new waypoints on the ND, including the vertical display. The KCCU also houses a keyboard with an alphabetic QWERTY keyboard, functional shortcuts, a thumbwheel, numeric pad, and backup curser control device (CCD).

Outboard of the PFD is the onboard information terminal (OIT), a database that includes everything from the aircraft's operating manual to navigation charts. Onboard information system (OIS) information is accessed and controlled using another keyboard, this one located on each pilot's pullout table. The keyboard only works with the OIM, but the crew can also use it to enter data on airport, aircraft, and weather so the system can calculate the takeoff and landing performance. These can then be passed straight on to the FMS which, in turn, sets the "bugs" (representing predetermined speeds) on the PFD.

The pilot's table is a feature unique to Airbus because of the space freed up by the use of side stick controllers in place of a conventional yoke. The side sticks provide pitch and roll control and, through the fly-by-wire flight-control system (FCS), command a piloting objective rather than a control surface position, a load factor for longitudinal control, and roll rate for lateral control.

This means that the pilot effectively moves the side stick in the desired direction, and the FCS evaluates the command and figures out the best way to achieve it using the combined control surfaces of the aircraft. The FCS consists of six flight control computers, each one of which is capable of controlling pitch, roll, and yaw axes through its associated actuators. To guarantee that no incipient problems crop up in either the hardware or software, the suite is made up of two dissimilar computer families with different technology, internal architecture, and software. The six are divided into three primary and three secondary computers, and the aircraft can be dispatched with any one if one of the six failed.

Software for the FCS, as well as all the other system software aboard, resides within the 32-unit Thales Avionics–supplied integrated modular avionics (IMA) suite, developed with Diehl. The IMA suite is made up of standardized electronic boards and modules and uses a common ARINC 653 operating system, providing a common module processing resource that several functions can share.

The IMA open-architecture concept enables software upgrades to be easily loaded into modules without the need for physically removing or replacing them. Cockpit, energy, cabin, and utility functions wholly or partly implemented in the IMA include the following: management of engine bleed, air-pressure control, air ventilation, avionics ventilation control, temperature control, air generation, flight warning, weight and balance back-up computation, air traffic communication, electrical load management, fuel management and measurement, brake and steering control, and several undercarriage-related functions. The IMA modules are connected with each other and the flight deck using the Rockwell Collins AFDX Ethernet systems bus.

On each wing, three ailerons and outboard spoilers provide roll control. For maximum redundancy, two actuators power each aileron, one servo controlled in the conventional way and the other by EHA. In normal operations, the servo control takes the lead, with the EHA simply damping. A single servo powers the spoilers apart from two (5 and 6), which are EBHA driven. Note the enormous size of the spoilers, which vary in area from 35.8 square feet inboard to almost 30 square feet outboard. *Mark Wagner*

Final checks on systems, including the auxiliary power unit (APU), went on around the clock through March and into April 2005 as Airbus made feverish preparations for first flight. One of the main focuses was on the electrical system, which, on an aircraft the size of the superjumbo, was large enough to supply a small town. Four variable-frequency generators are installed on each engine and deliver a nominal power of 150 kVA. Up to 120 kVA can be supplied by two constant-frequency generators on the APU, the access doors to which are seen open in this pre-first-flight shot. *Mark Wagner*

On touchdown the sturdy, six-wheeled Goodrich main gear legs can each withstand a load of more than 368,000 pounds—the equivalent of more than two fully loaded A320s! Parts for the gear are produced at Goodrich's facilities at Oakville, Ontario, Canada; Cleveland, Ohio; Tullahoma, Tennessee; and Krosno, Poland. *Mark Wagner*

Three ailerons and outboard spoilers provide roll control, with each aileron powered by two actuators that are either servo-controlled or controlled by electro-hydrostatic actuators (EHAs). Two also are driven by a separate form of actuator, the electric backup hydraulic actuator (EBHA). The two developments have stemmed from "more-electric" technology advances, and are crucial to the flight-control function in all three major axes. The EHAs convert electrical power into hydraulic power locally through an electric motor and a pump that moves a piston jack. The hydraulics within the EHA are totally independent of the aircraft's hydraulic system and are the first of their kind to be used commercially. The EBHAs, on the other hand, are used mainly as a safety backup and remain connected to the main hydraulic system, only transitioning to the electrical power supply in the event of a failure.

Pitch is controlled with a trimmable stabilizer with a powerful Ratier-Figeac 5,000-psi actuator and four elevators that are each actuated by one servo control and one EHA. Two rudders provide yaw control, with each section activated by two EBHAs from independent hydraulic and electrical systems. In case of hydraulic failure, the actuators concerned automatically revert to electrical mode, providing reduced speed but full deflection performance.

One of two independent hydraulic circuits power all flight-control surfaces. In addition, one of the two independent electrical circuits can power all surfaces,

except some spoilers and the outboard ailerons. Eaton is supplying the 5,000-psi hydraulic system—including eight engine-driven pumps, hydraulic lines, and hoses. Messier-Bugatti is supplying the hydraulic fluid collectors and filters, as well as the EHAs.

The hydraulics consist of two fully independent systems that are coded green and yellow, respectively. The priority supply is to flight controls and brakes, through priority and pressure-maintaining valves. The major consumers such as the landing gears and brake systems have an electrical backup power source through a system dubbed "LEHGS" (local electrical hydraulic generation system). The green system powers the nose and wing gears, while the yellow system powers the body gears.

The six-wheel body landing gear bogie is rearward retracting, while the two rear wheels mounted at the end of the 13-foot-long bogie beam are steerable up to 16 degrees but have no brakes. The four-wheel wing landing gear bogie folds inboard, while the two-wheel nose landing gear is forward retracting. The body-mounted main gear, developed by Goodrich, measures 16 feet tall from wheel base to retraction point, while the wing main gear, derived from the existing A340 design, is enlarged and fitted with a 10-foot-long shock strut outer cylinder. The Messier-Dowty nose gear also stands about 16 feet tall from the ground to the top of the drag stay.

Goodrich is the largest single subcontractor on the A380 and supplies not only the main gear and primary and secondary FCS, but also several structural items: the cargo mechanical system, exterior lighting, emergency evacuation system (see Chapter 13), and the primary and secondary air data systems. This provides information for the flight controls, flight deck displays, and standby instruments, and uses the company's SmartProbe multifunction sensing probe technology.

Goodrich has also developed, through its Aerolec joint venture with Thales Avionics Electrical Systems, the first variable frequency (VF) electrical power generation system to be used on a commercial aircraft of this size. The power comes from four VF generators, one installed per engine, that will provide 150 kVA in the 370- to 770-Hz range, while two 120-kVA constant-frequency generators are installed on the Pratt & Whitney Canada PW980A auxiliary power unit (APU) in the tail cone.

A generator driven by a drop-down Hamilton Sundstrand–developed ram-air turbine (RAT) can supply emergency AC power up to 90 kVA. The 62.5-inch-diameter RAT is 58 percent larger than any previous emergency turbine developed by the company and is the first all-electric RAT for Airbus.

High-pressure air, bled from the engines and the APU load compressor, is used to provide pneumatic pressure for air conditioning, wing anti-icing, engine starting, hydraulic-reservoir pressurization, and onboard oxygen generator system.

Hamilton Sundstrand–developed air generation system (AGS) machines, each with four stages, control the cabin environment, a major challenge with an aircraft capable of seating 840 in a high-density layout. The dual two-spool AGS units are housed in front of the wing box in the unpressurized area of the fuselage by the wing root and take in cold ram air before passing it through the heat exchangers. A central premixing unit combines the fresh air from the AGS with recirculation air flows. The pre-mixed air is then sent to the different cabin zones, where the flow is the equivalent of 0.66 pound/minute for an all-tourist-class layout, or 0.55 pound/minute for a high-density cabin.

Pressurization equal to 7,000 feet altitude up to 41,000 feet cruising altitude is provided by a quadruplex-synchronous control system that Hamilton subsidiary Nord-Micro developed. Four outflow valves are installed to minimize longitudinal airflow within the cabin in case of a valve failure, with two valves positioned in the lower forward fuselage and two in the lower aft.

Another equally massive environmental challenge for an aircraft of this capacity and range is providing an adequate water and waste disposal system. Potable water will be stored in up to eight tanks for a total volume of 600 gallons, though the baseline configuration is for six tanks. The water is carried along four main distribution mains, or lines, with two lines per deck. Waste water from the wash basins is vented overboard via drain masts.

Trash from the galleys is churned through waste disposal units and dumped into the vacuum toilet system.

The trimmable horizontal stabilizer can be moved through a range of minus 10 degrees and plus two. Elevator movement, on the other hand, is capable through a much wider range of minus 30 degrees to plus 20 degrees. As with the rudder, the elevators are split for multiple redundancy. The elevators on the left side are powered by the green hydraulic system, while those on the right are powered by the yellow. In addition to the standard servo-control actuator, each of the split elevators can also be controlled by an EHA. Note the nonstandard square panels of "sacrificial" skin and tail skid attachment added to protect the aft lower fuselage from potential damage during low-speed takeoff evaluations in flight test. *Mark Wagner*

The waste from the toilets also is transported through the same system to four collecting tanks with a combined capacity of just over 600 gallons. The tanks, which are equipped with fill level measuring devices, are located in the aft part of the aircraft by the bulk cargo hold and are fed by four vacuum toilet lines, with two lines per deck.

Emergency escape from the A380 has been a primary design driver since the start of concept definition. The sheer size required several innovations, including the unique main deck door 3 esca[...] it deploys in less than six seconds to fall beneath the slides from the upper deck and doors 4 and 5. The slide for door 3 is housed in the belly fairing. *Mark Wagner*

13
Turbulent Times

Not surprisingly, given its record-breaking size, the A380 project was no stranger to controversy as Airbus faced big questions over safety, weight, and cost, as well as the ability of airports to cope with the behemoth.

To Airbus, safety was paramount and had been the driving force behind the basic structural and systems redundancy of the design. Yet, as the A3XX became the A380, the issue was as much about public perception as it was certification. In fact, as the design was finalized, it became clear that there would be fewer potential certification issues with the new double-decker than with the pioneering fly-by-wire A320 of the previous decade.

It was to the traveling public, as much as to the operators and regulatory authorities, that Airbus wanted to demonstrate that the A380 would be fundamentally no different from anything before it. In fact, in terms of scale, the capacity increase of the 550-seat A380 over the 747 at between 35 and 40 percent, depending on configuration, was insignificant compared with the 100 percent increase seen with the introduction of the first 375-seat jumbos over the 150-seat 707.

Nevertheless, to satisfy certification requirements, Airbus still faced the daunting task of proving that the double-decker could be evacuated within 90 seconds using only half the available exits. Furthermore, to enable the certification basis to cover higher-capacity versions up to almost 900 seats, Airbus decided that nothing less than an evacuation demonstration would be performed with 873 people—20 crew and 853 passengers.

For the trial, more than 320 people would have to be evacuated through only three of the six doors on the upper deck. These escapees faced a descent of 27 feet to the ground.

The balance, more than 550 people (representing more than the standard maximum capacity of most of the initial operators) had to make their escape through five of the 10 main deck exits.

Airbus put this all to the test in Hamburg, where the "passengers"—all volunteers from local sports and social clubs—gathered to represent the required mix of age and gender that the European Aviation Safety Agency (EASA) and the U.S. Federal Aviation Administration (FAA) stated. These agencies called for a minimum of 40 percent females, of whom 15 percent had to be over 50 years old. Overall, 35 percent of the total volunteer force had to be over 50.

For the test, conducted in a darkened hangar at Finkenwerder, the passengers slid to the ground on Goodrich-developed dual-lane slides. Each lane could handle up to 70 passengers per minute. To help overcome the chances of hesitancy by passengers at the top of the slide (particularly the upper deck), the slides were extra wide and projected farther out from the sides, making them appear less steep. Higher sidewalls and built-in illumination were also added to further reassure the passengers, while also improving the seaworthiness of the slides as rafts in case an aircraft needed to be ditched at sea.

The slides were a major feat of design engineering in their own right, being built to fully inflate in 6 seconds and to remain stable in a 25-knot wind from any direction, with all engines running at idle. Not only did they have to avoid the "noodling" effect seen on earlier wide-body escape slides, including the upper-deck escape system of the original 747, but they had to be long enough to reach the ground even in the case of the aircraft ending up nose up or down. In the case of the A380, this made a big difference. The main-deck forward door sill height was only 9 feet above ground if the nose gear collapsed, but a rather more giddy 32 feet above ground if it rocked back on its tail.

To help plan for the best location of exits, Airbus commissioned a leading aircraft evacuation safety expert, Professor Edward Galea of the United Kingdom's Greenwich University. Galea specialized in developing computer-based models that allowed users

to study the impact on safety of the various design options. Data from the models, derived in part from live evacuation trials at Cranfield University, also in the United Kingdom, helped prove that the final exit and cabin configurations would satisfy the 90-second rule.

The Cranfield work in particular showed that the best way to guarantee the safest passenger flow toward an exit on any airliner—and not just the A380—was to increase the space between the galley or lavatory bulkheads. Often stationed as "monuments" by an exit, the research showed that the optimum width between these units was the 30 inches already used in the A380, against the required minimum of 20 inches. Overall, the aircraft boasted 16 emergency exits, with eight each side. The main deck had four double-width slides, a single overwing slide that deployed aft, and three wide upper-deck slides.

Weighty Matters

Like all aircraft manufacturers, Airbus waged a constant battle with weight in all its new aircraft, and the A380 was no exception. Unlike anything before it, however, the sheer scale of the superjumbo meant that seemingly minor changes such as over-designed parts or inaccurate sensors could have massive downstream

effects on weight. A 1 percent error in fuel calculation, for example, equated to the weight of 30 passengers.

Following the design changes implemented for QC/2 and the longer range requirements of Singapore Airlines and Qantas in 2000, the maximum takeoff weight inevitably ballooned to 1.23 million pounds, an increase of 35,000 pounds. The growth came from the added weight of the larger re-fanned engines, the add-on wing weight to carry them, the additional fuel volume, changes to the control surfaces for improved takeoff performance, and structural enhancement for the added weight in the fuselage and undercarriage.

Weight adds weight, and very soon the situation threatened to get out of hand, creating a potential dis-

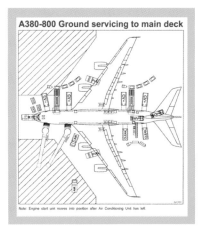

A380-800 Ground servicing to main deck

Note: Engine start unit moves into position after Air Conditioning Unit has left.

Ground handling and servicing were designed to be as routine as any other large aircraft, and with the exception of the oil filling port for the APU high in the tail cone, few servicing duties require special ground equipment. The photo illustrates the relative positions of the many service vehicles that would be used to help turn around an A380. It also shows loading and unloading using only two passenger bridges from the terminal to the main deck, which, for a full load of 555 passengers, Airbus estimated would require a 126-minute turnaround time. This was based on a studied average boarding rate of 15 passengers per minute and a disembarkation rate of 25 per minute—proving that no matter how good the manufacturer believes the aircraft to be, the passengers still can't wait to get off! *Airbus*

To address upper deck access concerns for some airports and operators, Airbus set up the direct upper deck access (DUDA) committee in 2003. This helped establish the exact design criteria for advanced upper deck air bridges such as this version developed by Florida–based FMC Jetway. Although the same overall length as existing bridges, it is elevated to a height of 27 feet to reach U1, the upper deck door 7, and will work with a second bridge to reach the main deck (M2) door and even a third to access M1. Jetway's first upper deck bridges were sold to Sydney and Melbourne airports in Australia, which began installations in September 2005. *FMC Technologies - Jetway*

To help make the superjumbo more maneuverable on the ground, the rear axles of the six-wheel body landing gear were designed to be steerable in a similar fashion to those on the 777. The feature is active during taxiing and push back, and during towing only if electrical power is applied, generated by the aircraft or the tow truck. The rear two steerable wheels will not be fitted with brakes. *Mark Wagner*

aster for Airbus. Speaking in 2003, Charles Champion recalled the problems when he said that, "we had the idea to put the whole company in a crisis mode two years ago, and the pressure is still on." Tiger Teams aggressively pursued a massive series of weight-reduction initiatives that, at one stage, numbered almost 50. Several structural modifications such as the use of composite ribs in the wings were implemented as a result, while others were studied for potential future use. Suppliers also were asked to cut weight, particularly in areas such as interior fittings, where they were tasked with taking out up to a massive 20 to 30 percent. The overall weight reduction target was set at an astonishing 22,000 pounds.

Most observers used operating empty weight (OEW) as the baseline against which to judge the overall weight problem of the project, which officially grew from 588,000 pounds in early 2000 to 595,000 pounds in 2002 and almost 608,000 pounds in 2004. The airlines, however, revealed that Airbus was concerned that the true figures were actually higher: 608,000 pounds in 2000, 613,000 pounds in 2002, and 619,000 pounds in 2003. In fact, it was worse than that when late 2004 estimates showed that the real OEW would be a little below 639,000 pounds by the time the interior was completely fitted out.

Structurally, however, Airbus kept its sights firmly on the maximum weight empty (MWE), which was

the baseline weight of the completed airframe, engines, painted structure, systems, and undercarriage. Internally, Airbus was also convinced that its Tiger Teams could claw back the OEW specification to 596,000 pounds and added confidently in 2004 that the launch customers would be comfortable with the OEW of the first aircraft.

Operator's items adding to the weight included 1,600 pounds of unusable fuel, 460 pounds of oil for the engines and APU, 3,750 pounds of water for the galleys and lavatories, plus 160 pounds of waste-tank treatment chemicals, 100 pounds of aircraft documents and tool kit, 19,700 pounds for seats, around 17,500 pounds of catering, another 7,700 pounds for the galley and other structures, plus 4,390 for the escape slides and other emergency equipment. The crew, including two pilots and 20 attendants and their luggage, added a further 3,700 pounds.

This additional weight added up to almost 60,000 pounds and, when subtracted from the OEW, gave an esti-mated MWE of just over 536,000 pounds. This was the key figure, because it meant that Airbus would still be able to meet its contractual specified empty weight even if it did not meet its target OEW. Additionally, the weight equated to payload and range, and there-fore performance. Despite all the weight issues, Airbus remained adamant that it would meet performance guarantees from the start, including the ability to reach 35,000 feet within 200 nautical miles and 30 minutes of brake release.

To cover the potential for excess growth in the MWE, Airbus studied a 19,800-pound optional increase in maximum takeoff weight in December 2003. Airbus said that the extra weight could be used for either range or payload increases, but was reticent about commenting on the true nature of the weight problem.

However, some better news began to come in during early 2004 with the start of subassembly pro-duction and the advent of additional weight-saving initiatives. Although too late for incorporation into the first three aircraft, several could be built into the fourth airframe (MSN007), which would also be refit-

The complex packaging of the hefty gear, and the resulting close proximity of the wing landing gear and body landing gear during retraction, is illustrated in this Goodrich graphic. *Goodrich*

Although this might look like a crew working on a road under construction, it is actually the start of Airbus' full-scale pavement tests that were begun in 1998 to validate the A3XX/A380 landing gear design as well as anticipate future runway loading classification techniques. The white-wheeled objects represent the main undercarriage, with the inner pair being the body landing gear and the outer the wing landing gear. The red structures to the left are massive weights designed to simulate the maximum ramp weight of more than 1.2 million pounds at maximum aft center of gravity, or the worst case scenario. The marked-out taxiway area to the right is part of the specially instrumented "flexible" pavement built to measure the loading. *Airbus*

ted for eventual sale to SIA. These changes included the use of GLARE for leading edges of the tail and would later be retrofitted to the MSN002 and -004. The changes also meant that the higher weight option was no longer vital to meet guarantees, making it an extra-cost option.

Airports Prepare

Boeing, rather than Airbus, began to warn airports to prepare for the advent of very large aircraft when it addressed the Airports Council International (ACI) meeting in Switzerland in 1994. Boeing forecast that airports such as Tokyo, Hong Kong, Taipei, and Osaka, in particular, would need to handle thousands of high-capacity transports per year from about 2010 onward.

Airbus surveyed a variety of airports around the world where it expected the A380 to see service. The airports were selected on the basis of the route struc-tures or regular destinations of the key carriers that had already either ordered the A380 or had made expressions of interest. By 2003, the tally reached 86

135

airports, including 32 Asia-Pacific airports, 15 in Europe, 18 in the United States, and a spread of 21 in destinations as varied as Argentina, Brazil, Canada, India, Mexico, the Middle East, Pakistan, Sri Lanka, and South Africa.

Priority went to the airports where the first wave of A380s would begin operation in 2006 and 2007. These included Bangkok, Paris Charles de Gaulle, Dubai, Frankfurt, Hong Kong, Jeddah, New York JFK, Kuala Lumpur, Los Angeles, London's Heathrow and Gatwick Airports, Melbourne, Montreal, Tokyo Narita, San Francisco, Singapore, and Sydney. The next wave, from 2008 to 2009, was expected to include the big cargo hubs at Anchorage; Indianapolis; Memphis; Ontario, California; as well as Kansai, Shanghai, and Taipei. Other potential early destinations beyond phase two included Auckland, Amsterdam, Beijing, Minneapolis/St. Paul, Nice, Paris Orly, Toronto, Vancouver, and Zurich.

In working so closely with the airports, Airbus was promoting the high-capacity, high-efficiency value equation that formed the foundation of the A380 concept. The message was simply that the A380 was part of the solution to the growing congestion, rather than the problem itself. Airbus argued that adapting to the ultra-high-capacity aircraft was a more efficient use of ramp and runway space than developing extra runways and gates to handle a larger number of smaller aircraft. Airbus also determined that the cost of adapting to the A380 would be relatively small compared to the roughly $20 billion per year airports of the world spend on general upgrades.

Using data from a group of 30 airports originally surveyed by ACI, Airbus predicted that adaptation costs would be about $100 million each for taxiway and apron improvements, strengthening of taxiway and culvert bridges, and terminal upgrades, including the development of double-deck air bridges. Airbus said that, "about 200 airports accept the 747 today. As aircraft capacity has not changed for more than three decades, it is time to prepare for the future."

Not all agreed with this analysis, particularly in the United States, where the spending watchdog, the GAO (General Accounting Office), estimated in 2002 that the 14 North American airports most likely to handle the A380 would have to spend about $2.1 billion, or an average of at least $150 million each. Airbus challenged the findings, saying they were "not the result of detailed analysis, but rather reflect extremely rough and inconsistent estimating." By contrast, Airbus calculated that U.S. airports would need to spend about $520 million, or just under a quarter of the GAO's estimates. This was partly because Airbus identified costs in the GAO's estimates that would have been spent on modernization and capacity improvement anyway.

Most of the estimated costs were associated with the wider taxiways and runways that the GAO said would be needed for the A380, which the FAA classed as a Group VI aircraft. This included extending the width of runways to 200 feet and taxiways to 98 feet, the latter only being required to be 75 feet wide for Group V aircraft such as the 747. However, as Airbus pointed out, the landing gear footprint of the A380 was less than 46 feet, meaning that it would still be able to use the standard Code E (75-foot-wide) taxiway as long as the shoulders were extended by 61 feet on each side. This would take overall taxiway width to 197 feet, compared to the minimum 144 feet typically required for the 747.

The distance between the nose gear and the aftermost main gear—the six-wheel body-mounted undercarriage units—was just over 104 feet, or roughly 20 feet longer than the 747. However, when measured to the steering point around which the A380 turned, the axis was just over 97 feet, making it slightly less than the 100-foot steering axis of the 777-300 and the 108 feet of the A340-600. Airports around the world had already adapted to these other giants by

adding fillets to runway access taxiways and other areas where maneuvers could be limited, so Airbus was certain that this aspect would not be a problem.

To work out how the enormous weight of the A380, and particularly that of the 1.3-million-pound -800F freighter version, would impact runway and taxiway surfaces, Airbus built a curious contraption called the landing gear configuration test vehicle. Laden with heavy weights, the skeletal vehicle rolled along on 20 wheels to simulate the pavement loading of the A380. As well as maneuvering around, the vehicle was rolled over a special flexible pavement area that was laid down at Toulouse with weight-sensing instruments built into the concrete and asphalt. Using the data, Airbus discovered that the A380's ACN (Aircraft Classification Number—an ICAO method of calculating the load-bearing value of an aircraft) was between 66 and 72, compared to 69 for the 747, as much as 75 for the A340-600, 83 for the 777-300ER, and 69 for the 767-400ER.

The use of a static load on a slowly moving trolley-like device to simulate the aircraft was sometimes questioned but was perfectly valid. A general misconception

Another critical destination for the aircraft early on in its career was Los Angeles International (LAX), which was expected to handle as many as nine A380 flights a day as early as 2008. Although widely criticized early on for apparently dragging its heels on preparations, the airport authority quickly gathered pace with a massive $11 billion expansion plan beginning in the mid-2000s. The scheme included special gates at the Tom Bradley International terminal and a bespoke "mini-terminal" in the north area of the remote parking site dedicated to A380s. A typically busy day at LAX is captured in this image of United's bustling Terminals 6 and 7. *Mark Wagner*

Airbus was considered nothing more than a minor annoyance to Boeing until Airbus' landmark sale of 23 A300B4s to Eastern Airlines in 1978. The deal sent shockwaves through the industry, conferred a new level of credibility on Airbus, and triggered investigations by three subcommittees of the U.S. Congress into what would later explode into the long-running subsidies row. *Mark Wagner*

Within days of the Airbus board giving authority to offer the A3XX in 2000, the U.S. government demanded details of German and U.K. government funding for the project to determine if they complied with World Trade Organization (WTO) rules. Development costs at this stage were expected to be up to $12 billion, of which 33 percent could come from the partner governments as reimbursable loans under the terms of the 1992 Large Civil Airliner (LCA) agreement between the United States and the European Union. This aid was repayable over 17 years at or above the cost of government borrowing. At the start of 2005, Airbus said initial research and development was estimated at €10.7 billion (U.S. $12.4 billion), plus the potential for a further €1.45 billion (U.S. $1.69 billion) "overrun" between then and the planned completion of the A380 development program (including freighter derivatives) in 2011. *Mark Wagner*

was that the greatest load is experienced by the runway surface when an aircraft lands. But the actual impact weight is about 50 percent of the total weight, as the aircraft wing is still producing lift, and the weight is gradually transferred to the wheels as the aircraft slows down. Conversely, the weight on takeoff gradually decreases as the aircraft accelerates and lift increases. The most critical weight situation is when the aircraft is fully loaded and static on the ramp, or when it is slowly moving toward takeoff.

Turnaround time, or the period needed to offload the passengers, service the aircraft, and board the next passenger load, was also a critical concern. Airbus believed that the fundamental design of the A380 cabin architecture would be the key to smooth operations and quick turnaround times and placed its faith in the positioning of the two forward main deck doors and the stairway to the upper deck. "This results in a more balanced door utilization in comparison to the 747 where, although there are two doors, the majority of passengers board through door 2," said Airbus. The design caused congestion because, Airbus said, most airlines used door 1 for first and business class only on the 747, and even in the unrestricted use of door 1,

Airbus said the design caused delays as "flow to the aft of the cabin is choked by congestion in the door 2 area due to back-queuing of passengers on the narrow stairs to the upper deck."

With the A380 design, passengers on the upper deck and first-class main deck area were expected to load through door 1, while the bulk of main deck passengers would load through door 2. Referenced against a typical 747-400 turnaround time of 85 minutes with 417 passengers and two bridges, the A380 was expected to be turned around in about 90 minutes with 555 passengers and two bridges, plus a trolley lift at door 2 to help with upper deck catering. If main-deck-only catering and other services were used, the time was extended to 126 minutes. The time was shortened considerably to 80 to 85 minutes if the airport was using three bridges and upper deck servicing via the upper deck door 1 on the right side.

The airports themselves ramped up steadily to prepare for the aircraft on services from 2006 onward. Key locations such as New York, San Francisco, and Los Angeles were in the forefront of the major group of 11 phase one North American destinations that declared themselves ready for the aircraft by 2005. In Europe, 10 airports were ready by the same time, while a further 30 spread across the Middle East, Asia, and the Pacific region also declared themselves prepared for the giant aircraft by the middle of 2005.

In Europe, Eryl Smith, the planning and development director for British Airports Authority (BAA) Heathrow, told the press in July 2004 that, "the Airbus A380 is critical for us—it will change the face of Heathrow and the face of long-haul travel. Building for the A380 is the right thing to do." The airport completely rebuilt Terminal 3's pier 6 to provide four double-deck A380 stands under a $180 million scheme, with an additional four stands and three gates planned for Terminal 4 from mid-2006, and five additional A380 stands designed for the new Terminal 5 by 2011. Overall, the airport expects to have 14 A380-capable stands by 2016, when it expects that A380s would operate one in every eight long-range flights. Meanwhile, Munich Airport in Germany became the first in Europe to gain formal ICAO Category F classification to handle the A380 in early 2004.

To prepare for the A380 in New York, the JFK board of commissioners authorized $179 million worth of upgrades in April 2004. Bill DeCota, aviation director of JFK's operating group, the Port Authority of New York and New Jersey, said the investment was worthwhile because "the arrival of the A380 is as important to JFK International Airport as

the Boeing 747 was when it was introduced. There's a huge economic benefit to seeing an aircraft like that in a market like ours."

On the West Coast, San Francisco took the lead in making preparations, becoming one of the first airports in the United States to obtain full FAA certification for its A380-adapted terminal and airfield changes. The airport's director, John Martin, said, "We planned for the future by designing the new international terminal to accommodate the new large aircraft, such as the A380, and that just makes sense, given we have 50 daily nonstop flights to 27 international cities, many of which will be served by the A380."

In Los Angeles, which was expected to handle up to nine A380s a day by 2008, things were moving more slowly because of budget problems and political infighting within the governing city council. In late 2003, Virgin Atlantic Chairman Sir Richard Branson said, "Los Angeles [LAX] has been the slowest of all the early A380 airports to get its act together. I have written to [California governor] Arnold Schwarzenegger to ask him to intervene."

Virgin Atlantic later delayed its A380 deliveries because of worries over interior configurations and concerns over preparations at LAX—one of its key destinations. LAX meanwhile stepped up its plans, which included modifying two gates at the Tom Bradley International Terminal as well as double-bridge jet bridges at multiple remote gates at the west end of the airfield where it intended to develop a mini-terminal for A380s by 2010–2011. Overall, however, LAX was confident that the go-ahead of an $11 billion airport expansion plan in early 2005 meant it could catch up and be ready for the first arrivals of the big jet in late 2006.

Subsidy Storm

As its first flight approached, the A380 entered the eye of a new storm over unfair government support that had raged on and off between the Europeans and the Americans since the late 1970s. Although U.S. manufacturers had considered Airbus inconsequential for almost a decade, they were forced to sit up and take notice following the Eastern Airlines A300B order in 1978.

Urged on by the U.S. manufacturers, Washington trade representatives took up the issue with their European counterparts, and the following year an agreement was signed to remove trade barriers on civil aircraft. The agreement did not limit subsidies, however, and, in 1989, the issue once again flared up when

At Farnborough 2004, the war of words erupted over subsidies once more between Airbus and Boeing. Airbus Chief Executive Noel Forgeard accused Boeing of having a hidden agenda when it came to raising the rhetoric on subsidies during a presidential election year when job outsourcing was a hot political potato in the United States. Boeing, on the other hand, said it wanted the bilateral agreement re-examined because it was never intended to be a permanent agreement. *Mark Wagner*

the West German government promised to protect Messerschmitt Bolkow Blohm (MBB) from extreme currency fluctuations. Under its plan, the Airbus partner, by then owned by Daimler-Benz, would get a $2.6 billion subsidy if the U.S. dollar exchange rate fell below DM 1.6.

The battle threatened to erupt in an all-out transatlantic trade war that was only averted after long drawn-out negotiations that resulted in a 1992 bilateral agreement on subsidies for the development of large civil aircraft (LCA). The agreement limited direct support to 33 percent of development costs. Twenty-five percent of this was to be at an interest rate no lower than the government's cost of borrowing, with the remainder at a rate 1 percent higher. The loans also had to be repaid within 17 years, while the benefits of the indirect support (loosely defined as reductions in research-and-development costs resulting from government-funded civil and military research work) were also limited to 4 percent of any of the company's annual commercial turnover.

The agreement worked well in principle but not in practice for two main reasons. First, no true definition was agreed to as to what exactly "indirect support" meant. Second, there were no means of enforcing any of the provisions of the agreement, which instead relied on biannual meetings to review all publicly available information on direct and indirect government support. The agreement also called for a progressive reduction in launch aid, but again this was not clearly defined.

By 2001, with the LCA agreement nearing 10 years old, the A380 launched, Airbus gobbling up a unprecedented amount of market share, and the Sonic Cruiser project emerging, Boeing began to review the subsidy issue once more. Its research revealed that Airbus had received at least $15 billion in government subsidies since the start of the 1970s, and it believed that the low interest and lenient repayment terms for one-third of the estimated $12 billion A380 development costs had effectively allowed it to make a convincing business case for launching it in the first place.

In addition, Boeing questioned whether the launch aid for the A380 even fell within the bounds of the LCA agreement, which it said had been violated through state and local infrastructure improvements in France, Germany, Spain, and the United Kingdom. Furthermore, Boeing claimed that the LCA agreement had been biased in favor of Airbus, which was then a start-up company requiring some sort of protection. When the deal was negotiated, Airbus was delivering just 20 percent of the world's civil aircraft. By 2001, the picture was quite different, with Airbus taking more orders than Boeing. By 2003, Airbus had taken the lead in both orders and deliveries.

Leading the rhetoric was Harry Stonecipher, the former chief executive of Boeing. Speaking to *Flight International* in 2004, he said, "As soon as it came to launching the A380, then all the hosepipes were hooked up to the treasuries of three countries in particular and $4 billion came zooming through. This whole subsidization thing has gone on long enough. They keep trying to turn it into a globalization issue. But this is about transparency and subsidy."

Europe, naturally, saw quite another side of the coin, particularly by 2004, when Boeing was preparing the ground for launch of the 787. All along, Airbus maintained that Boeing (and before the merger, McDonnell Douglas) has benefited directly and indirectly from massive U.S. government aeronautical engineering research-and-development spending with NASA and the Department of Defense (DoD). Representatives of the European aviation industry believed that Boeing still received indirect government support through reimbursement of independent research and development money by the U.S. Defense Advanced Research Projects Agency (DARPA) and the DoD, and estimated the company had received $18 billion in indirect support since 1992.

EADS, with 80 percent of the newly relaunched Airbus, also countered with claims that any advantage from lower interest rates on the collective €4.3 billion (U.S. $5 billion) of government loans on its books, worked out at about $100,000 to $120,000 per aircraft. Given the multimillion-dollar price tag of the Airbus range, this was considered as the proverbial drop in the bucket.

At the 2004 Farnborough Air Show, the dispute about government subsidies became highly volatile with both sides firing salvo after salvo at each other. Airbus Chief Executive Noel Forgeard accused Boeing of having a hidden agenda, and that all the noise over subsidies was designed to stir anti-Airbus sentiment in the United States ahead of the award of key U.S. defense contracts. Boeing responded by saying that the agreement was out of date and sloppy.

By October 2004, the pot boiled over, with Airbus and Boeing both filing complaints to the World Trade Organization (WTO) over alleged abuses of the 1992 agreement. In a nutshell, Airbus wanted to see tighter controls on indirect support for Boeing, elimination of the tax breaks that Boeing received from the state of Washington to secure the location of the 7E7 (later 787), and fairer access to the U.S. defense market. Boeing, on the other hand, wanted to stop any more government loans to cover A380 cost overruns, and no more launch aid for any new Airbus programs.

It was the latter issue that caused problems in the talks, particularly after October 2004, when the United States decided to terminate the 1992 bilateral agreement and filed a formal complaint over illegal subsidies to Airbus with the World Trade Organization. The European Union responded with an immediate counterclaim alleging that Boeing had been receiving similar illegal subsidies from the U.S. government.

"The U.S. move in the WTO concerning European support for Airbus is obviously an attempt to divert attention from Boeing's self-inflicted decline," said EU Trade Commissioner Pascal Lamy. "If this is the path the U.S. has chosen, we accept the challenge, not least because it's high time to put an end to massive illegal U.S. subsidies to Boeing which damage Airbus, in particular those for Boeing's new 7E7 program." Robert Zoellick, the U.S. trade representative, retorted the move was "about fair competition and a level playing field. Some Europeans have justified subsidies to Airbus as necessary to support an industry in its infancy. If that rationalization were ever valid, its time has long since passed."

As the dispute rolled into 2005, now with new EU Trade Commissioner Peter Mandelson at the head of the European delegation, it threatened to become the most expensive trade dispute in WTO history. It also looked likely to entangle the Japanese government, which had openly subsidized its own manufacturers, which, in turn, took large contracts for the new 787 program. The intensity grew with preparations for the launch of the A350, the Airbus countermove to the 787 that Boeing had both expected and feared. At the time of the A380's first flight, it seemed as if a full-blown trade war could well be looming on the horizon. Some hope emerged at the 2005 Paris Air Show, however, when Airbus delayed the industrial go-ahead of the A350 until later that year. Both sides hoped the move would give time for a negotiated settlement through the WTO.

The emergence of the A350 as a challenger to Boeing's 787 "Dreamliner" helped reignite the subsidies row between Europe and the United States. The €4 billion (U.S. $5.3 billion) program, based on the successful A330 twinjet, won Airbus board approval in December 2004. For once it seems both Airbus and Boeing agree, roughly speaking, on the size of the market for this mid-size category, which Airbus sees as being for about 3,100 aircraft worth $400 billion over the next 20 years. *Airbus*

The A300 and its A310 derivative became well-established freighters, particularly in the latter phases of their respective development lives. The cargo market sustained the A300-600 line well into freighters and went on to enjoy a useful life with operators such as FedEx. One of its aircraft, part of a batch acquired from Swissair and KLM, takes off at Orange County's John Wayne Airport in

2000s, while many A310s were converted to
...rnia. *Mark Wagner*

14
Supersized Freighter

To Airbus there was never even a question that the A380 would make a successful freighter. After all, a superjumbo that could comfortably carry up to 35 percent more passengers than the 747 would surely be the heir apparent to the role of king of the cargo liners.

The simple arithmetic behind the A380F was that the capacious airframe offered up to 50 percent more cargo volume than its erstwhile competitor and, with its high capacity, the aircraft could boast up to 33 percent more payload. The economics translated into 20 percent lower costs per pound of cargo and an attractive proposition to a market that has seen virtually uninterrupted growth for the last four decades. From early on, therefore, the real question over the launch of the freighter wasn't if, but when.

With the go-ahead of the A3XX from 1996 onward, freight operators and airlines with large cargo divisions played a major role in the regular customer focus group (CFG) meetings with Airbus. Cargolux, DHL, EVA Airways, FedEx, and UPS were among the 20 airlines involved in the first few meetings. Atlas also became a prominent member of the CFG club from 1999 onward, while airlines with significant cargo operations such as Air France, Lufthansa, ANA, JAL, and SIA maintained a consistent presence over the years.

It was at operators such as these that Airbus first pitched its most definitive freighter and combi (combination passenger/freighter) plans for the A3XX-100. These began to crystallize following two freighter/combi workshops held during 1997, one of which FedEx hosted in Memphis, Tennessee, and the other Cargolux co-hosted in Luxembourg.

143

Airbus originally hoped to get the go-ahead for the freighter variant of the A3XX in early 1999 and put it into service as early as 2005, 18 to 20 months after the airliner version. From 1997 onward, intensive work with cargo airlines began to define the superjumbo, which was the first Airbus freighter to be designed and launched in parallel with the passenger version. The sales pitch was relatively straightforward: "This aircraft will carry more cargo farther at lower cost than anything else on the market." *Airbus*

The A380-800F does not have the distinctive nose cargo door of the 747 because studies that Airbus conducted with operators revealed it was of "limited value." In particular, it said the design required at least 75 feet of extra valuable ramp space in front of the aircraft to accommodate the loading equipment. Airbus decided the feature was both costly and heavy, opting instead for side-loading doors. Simulations showed that with simultaneous loading of both upper and lower decks, the -800F could be turned around in 135 minutes, against 150 minutes for the 747. *Mark Wagner*

Airbus appeared mildly surprised at the high level of interest in the freighter variant and promptly invited EVA Airways to co-host another meeting in 1998 at which it hoped to further define an offering that, if sufficient enthusiasm was shown, could be launched by early 1999.

The earliest definitions for both variants were configured with a main-deck cargo door measuring 11 feet, 3 inches by 8 feet, 3 inches in the aft fuselage. The pure freighter would also have featured a cargo door located in the forward fuselage on the upper deck. In the combi mode, the aft section of the main passenger deck was to have been configurable as a freight deck with capacity for up to 15 7-foot, 8-inch by 10-foot, 5-inch cargo pallets. A further 11 pallets or 34 LD3 containers—the industry-standard belly hold cargo container—could have been carried on the two lower deck holds.

A nose door, similar to the 747 design, was considered for the A3XX but rejected because of the weight and drag penalties of having to raise the flight deck. Unlike the 747, which was designed with the upraised flight deck from the outset with the freighter derivative in mind, the A3XX had a mezzanine-level flight deck below the upper deck and above the main deck level. This conscious decision meant that the A3XX freighter could accommodate standard-sized pallets only and not the larger seagoing-sized containers.

The beauty of the double-deck arrangement, as far as Airbus saw it, was that a combi configured in this fashion could carry up to 11 pallets, or 77,100 pounds of cargo, on the main deck and *still* be able to take 380 passengers, plus 33,000 pounds of freight in the standard cargo compartment, over a range of more than 7,000 nautical miles. The full-freight version, on the other hand, could carry a massive 57 pallets against the 30 carried by the 747-400F. The main deck had space for 28 pallets, while 18 could be held on the upper deck and a further 11 on the lower level, creating a total potential cargo payload of about 330,400 pounds!

There was no doubting the awesome capacity, but at the EVA meeting in Taiwan and several following workshops it became clear to Airbus that the airlines wanted more range at maximum weight. The changes to the baseline design (see Chapter 6) helped the freighter design team, which, by April 1999, was able to offer the capability to carry the maximum 330,400-pound payload over 5,600 nautical miles. To the freighter community this was big news. Earlier concepts had sketched these sorts of ranges, but with

"only" 275,330 pounds, and not quite the step change over the 747 that was needed.

The change was enough to excite a new level of interest, and Philippe Jarry, vice president of market development for Airbus' large aircraft division, confirmed that, "a group of airlines are actually demanding that we make the freighter available really soon. We didn't think we'd have such a positive response." It later emerged that the late Michael Chowdry, the energetic chairman of Atlas Air, had even urged Airbus to launch the freighter before the passenger version.

Airbus did at least indicate for the first time that, given this level of interest, the -100F could become the second major derivative to follow the -100 passenger version, rather than the planned extended-range or stretched versions. "More and more I believe this will be so, but it will be market driven," Jarry said. The decision was not insignificant, bearing in mind the amount of structural beefing-up that would be needed to take the weight, which was the equivalent of roughly 1,500 passengers.

Boeing, as the dominant heavy-air-freight manufacturer with the 747-400F, was not about to give up its monopoly without a fight, and throughout late 1999 and into 2000 pushed a freighter version of its revised 747X Stretch. The key target was FedEx, which had been a consistent supporter of the A3XX.

FedEx had already signed a tentative expression of interest for up to 20 A3XX freighters, joining Emirates, which had similarly signed for two and had a permanent seat on the airline advisory board.

Boeing knew it had its work cut out for it and approached FedEx with an attractive offer for the freight carrier's initial requirement for up to eight air-

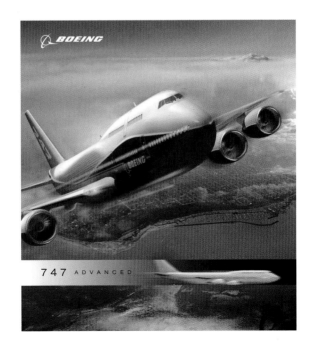

747 ADVANCED

FedEx plans to use its A380-800Fs on routes that traditionally demanded the use of two MD-11Fs a day, such as Memphis to Osaka Kansai, and Memphis to Paris. In effect, it would give the equal effect of putting two MD-11s into one fuselage, with a huge leap in efficiency as a result. The massive range capability of the aircraft also offers the potential to open up a series of new nonstop routes that were beyond the MD-11, such as Memphis to Hong Kong. At the same time, FedEx continued to stress its continued love of the MD-11, which it said the A380 would "augment" and not replace. *Mark Wagner*

craft. Boeing's game plan was relatively straightforward: offer a good price, promote the lower ton-mile operating costs it claimed, propose a faster delivery schedule, and push the fact that no new types of ground-cargo handling equipment would be needed

for the 747. Boeing also pointed out the interlining restrictions of the A3XX, which could not take 10-foot-tall pallets, as could the 747.

According to Boeing's predictions, the 747X Stretch freighter would have lower ton-per-mile costs

Airbus made several design changes to win a massive launch order for the A380-800F from FedEx, including a relatively late decision in 2000 to move the main deck cargo door 5 frames farther aft to improve ground handling. The carrier officially entered the A380 order book in July 2002 when it signed for 10 aircraft plus a further 10 options with first deliveries in 2008. A winning feature of the aircraft was its phenomenal freight capacity of 331,000 pounds combined with a range of 5,800 nautical miles that enabled it to cross the Pacific nonstop, eliminating expensive stopovers and a whole extra day from the all-important delivery time. *Mark Wagner*

than the A3XX-100F, largely because of the 747's lower empty weight. Using Airbus data, Boeing said, "the A3XX's upper cargo deck has a penalty of about 100,000 pounds operating empty weight, making its ton-per-mile direct operating costs 12 percent greater than the 747X Stretch freighter."

Boeing knew it still had a chance because FedEx had not been able to get an agreement on pricing with Airbus. The freighter market was also hot, particularly in Asia, where operators had led a rush on 747-400Fs, placing orders for more than 20 aircraft in only nine months. The area had seen a big bounce back from the Asian flu that had hit only three years earlier, seeing year-on-year double-digit air cargo traffic growth to pre-1997 levels. Boeing Cargo Marketing Regional Director James Edgar predicted that within a few years "more than half the world's entire 747-400F fleet will be domiciled in Asia."

Based on what it had seen with orders and market development, Boeing predicted annual air cargo growth from the late 1990s figure of about 180 billion revenue ton per km (RTK) to over 500 billion RTK by 2020. To carry all this, Boeing expected the world freighter fleet to almost double to 3,000 aircraft, of which 600 would be new, 1,800 converted, and 600 retained in service. Meanwhile, other operators, all of them loyal 747 freighter users, also were showing interest in the new Stretch proposal. Atlas Air, Lufthansa, and Polar Air had joined FedEx in discussions with Boeing.

In late October 2000, talks between Boeing and FedEx reached an advanced stage, and by early November, Boeing believed the deal was in the bag. To its dismay, however, Airbus came flying back to Memphis with a better offer and a better aircraft. Having re-emphasized the 1,260-nautical-mile range advantage it still claimed over the proposed 747X Stretch freighter, Airbus came back to FedEx with a sweeter deal. It had also relocated the main deck cargo door aft by five fuselage frames to improve ground handling.

The changes in price and configuration were enough to bring FedEx back to the Airbus camp and, probably just as important for Airbus, enough to stamp out the 747X Stretch and, with it, one of Boeing's last chances to puncture the balloon before its impending official launch. FedEx's decision to go with the Airbus was also a vital strategic step for the growth of the A3XX family, as the thicker wing skins and stronger landing gear would provide the basis for the extended-range passenger model, as well as lay the foundation for the stretched variant.

FedEx Launch Order

In early January 2001, the deal was confirmed when FedEx signed a memorandum of understanding for the newly named A380-800F. In signing up for 10 firm plus further options, FedEx became the seventh customer for the superjumbo and increased the overall backlog to 60. FedEx was also the first U.S. operator for the aircraft, as well as the first dedicated cargo airline to be a launch customer for the A380 freighter.

FedEx Chairman Fred Smith said that the A380-800F's 39,000 cubic feet of cargo space was a "quantum leap in size and capability" over the MD-11F and even the 747X Stretch which, he added, was "much smaller in terms of cubic space." Aside from the 331,000-pound payload, transpacific range, and an option for further growth variants, the deal also was allied to very keen pricing and negotiations over possibly accelerating deliveries that initially called for the aircraft to come into the fleet at the rate of three per year from 2008 onward.

Boeing said the FedEx loss was very disappointing but pressed on with briefing 21 other prospective customers at a cargo symposium in Seattle the same month. Atlas, Cathay Pacific, British Airways, Cargolux, and Lufthansa were all there, as was Air France, which was still showing interest in the 747 freighter, despite being an A380 launch customer. The FedEx loss, however, was a major blow from which the 747X Stretch effort never fully recovered, and within three months Boeing's development priorities had shifted to an altogether new focus—the Sonic Cruiser high-speed long-range 767 airliner replacement.

The move also signaled an end, at least for the moment, to Boeing's challenge of the A380. In a statement on March 29, 2001, the company said, "airline customers have indicated that, with continued improvements, the 747-400 family will satisfy the majority of their large airplane needs. Development of the Longer Range 747-400 (with optional auxiliary tanks and heavier structure) will continue; the first air-

plane will be delivered to Qantas in November 2002. Boeing is also studying additional improvements to the 747-400 and will protect its ability to develop a larger 747X, if and when customers indicate a need." Ironically, the subsequent abandonment of the Sonic Cruiser led to the more efficient 7E7 study in early 2003. This was later launched as the 787 Dreamliner with advanced engines that were also offered on a new version of the 747 dubbed the Advanced. In April 2005, just as the A380 was making its first flight, Boeing selected the General Electric GEnx engine for the 747 Advanced stretch, which was offered in both passenger and freighter versions. With a go/no-go choice to make by mid-2005, it was Boeing's last chance to extend the life of the venerable jumbo, with cargo carriers such as Cargolux tipped as potential customers.

In July 2002, FedEx officially firmed up its A380-800F order, declaring its intent to take three aircraft in 2008, three each in 2009 and 2010, and one in 2011. FedEx also confirmed options for another 10 aircraft. Fred Smith said the agreement "secures the most efficient, long-range aircraft in the world for the future needs of the FedEx fleet," and added that rather than flying several MD-11s between FedEx hubs in Europe, North America, and Asia, it "could operate a single A380 on those routes."

The next month, Airbus firmed up specifications for the freighter after more in-depth talks with FedEx and Emirates. The baseline entry-into-service aircraft was defined with a maximum takeoff weight (MTOW) of 1.3 million pounds, a range of 5,600 nautical miles, and a payload of 330,400 pounds. A

wide variety of potential future pathways were also open, however, which traded on various combinations of payload, takeoff weight, and range.

The top range was limited only by the MTOW, which, in turn, was limited by the design capabilities of the structure. Senior marketing analyst for the A380, Marie-Ange Plancq, said the MTOW could be increased to 1.43 million pounds on current design principles and would allow the development of up to three additional options. One would have more payload but less range, while another would feature an increased MTOW for greater range, and a third would have both a higher gross weight and extra fuel for ultra-long-range operations.

The increased payload would be able to lift more than 348,000 pounds, but with a range limited to about 3,000 nautical miles. For this version, the MTOW would be restricted to 1.18 million pounds, while the maximum zero fuel weight would be increased to 903,080 pounds from the baseline 885,460 pounds. The longer-range version would have an increased MTOW of almost 1.33 million pounds, but with a slightly reduced cargo capacity of 279,740 pounds and a design range of 6,900 nautical miles.

For extra-long-range operations, Airbus studied an optional 11,080-gallon center fuel tank that, when combined with the higher MTOW of the longer-range version, would be able to carry 204,845 pounds over ranges of up to 8,500 nautical miles. These options were to be studied as technical tradeoffs, and the baseline aircraft "has enough structural margin to cope with the MTOW increase without modifications of operating restrictions," said Plancq.

FedEx and Airbus meanwhile worked jointly to evaluate a series of new cargo loading systems capable of holding four containers, double the capacity of the current system. The target was a turnaround time of 90 minutes, or the same time it took to load and unload an MD-11. The sill of the main deck door, at 16 feet, 8 inches, would be accessible by standard 747 loading equipment, but the 26-foot-tall upper-deck door sill would require the development of new loaders. To complete preparations, the two also worked on transfer techniques between aircraft and based these on the standard 8-foot-tall FedEx wide-body container as well as the transfers for the narrow-body containers, which would fit on the upper deck.

By now, the side door size on the upper deck had been fixed at 12 feet by 7 feet, 4 inches, enabling up to 25 contoured 96-inch-by-125-inch-by-82-inch pallets to be loaded on and off. The main deck door was

increased to 14 feet by 9 feet, 3 inches, providing access for 33 96-inch-by-125-inch-by-96-inch pallets, while the belly hold, accessed via the standard cargo doors, housed seven 96-inch-by-125-inch-by-64-inch pallets in the forward hold and six in the aft. To provide sufficient vertical "tween" deck space, the freighter main deck floor would be slightly lower than the passenger version, and the ceiling would be slightly higher. This was possible through the removal of main deck seat rails and the use of aluminum rather than composites for the upper deck floor.

With the program momentum building through 2003, Singapore Airlines subsidiary SIA Cargo opened fact-finding talks with Airbus over the A380-800F. The talks went on into 2004 and included the potential switch of any of its 25 firm or option positions to freighters, but the talks clearly indicated the emergence of more interest from a key Asian airline.

Surprisingly, it was not Asia but the United States that provided the next big break for the A380 freighter when, just a week before the official public unveiling, or "reveal," of the aircraft, the express freight carrier UPS announced an order for 10 aircraft with options on a further 10. UPS had been involved in the customer focus group process since 1996 and had a key role in the definition of the A3XX/A380.

In the intervening years, UPS had also become a key customer of Airbus, having earlier placed a massive order for 90 A300-600Fs, and as part of the

A380F deal this order was reduced to 53. This meant that UPS would take its last A300-600F in July 2006 and its first A380F in 2009. The $2.2 billion transaction was well worth it to Airbus, which welcomed UPS as the 14th customer for the A380.

Assembly of the first freighter was expected to begin by the end of 2006, with first flight in 2007 and entry into service with FedEx in the second quarter of 2008. With a fairly rapid freighter fleet build-up expected through the first five years of production, it seems that the awesome spectacle of the A380-800F will become a familiar sight at cargo hubs around the world by 2015.

Behind the glamour and glitz of the lavish reveal ceremony at the Jean-Luc Lagardére final assembly line on January 18, 2005, was a growing sense of urgency to get going with the flight test ar
massive celebration of a remarkable achievement and a fitting way to mark not only the unveiling of the largest airliner ever built, but also the passing of 2004 as one of the best years yet in Airb
had delivered 320 aircraft, or just over 53 percent of all the new 100-plus seaters delivered worldwide. It also beat Boeing in the order books in 2004, taking 370 new firm orders, or 57 percent, w

15

The New Space Age Begins

Oblivious to the driving rain and cold winds howling outside, 4,500 guests were snug inside the gargantuan final assembly hall in Toulouse on January 18, 2005, to witness the grand reveal of the A380 to the world.

Fireworks, illuminated fountains, music, and light enthralled the crowd as a narrator spelled out the story of the A380 through a series of projected images on giant screens. Finally, the moment everyone had been waiting for arrived when four children pressed a button to raise an enormous blue curtain to reveal the aircraft in its new blue-and-white Airbus livery.

After the spontaneous cheers and applause died away, the collected government leaders of the four partner countries heaped praise on the achievements of the company. "It is a technological feat and a great European success," said French President Jacques Chirac who added that "when it takes to the skies, it will carry the colors of our continent and our technological ambitions to even greater heights."

British Prime Minister Tony Blair described the aircraft as "simply stunning," and added, "This is the most exciting new aircraft in the world, a symbol of economic strength and technical innovation. Above all, it is a symbol of confidence that we can compete and win in the global market." With the recently ignited transatlantic subsidies row obviously in mind, German Chancellor Gerhard Schroeder could not resist the temptation to snipe at the United States when he said the multinational project had been accomplished because of the "tradition of good old Europe."

In the first week of April, with the schedule already tight, MSN001 was handed over to the Airbus flight test division to make preparations for the first flight. Everywhere she went around the perimeters of Toulouse's Blagnac Airport, the massive aircraft was a crowd puller! *Airbus*

Basically an empty shell during initial testing, the interior of MSN001's upper deck reveals the rows of water tanks required to ballast the aircraft for flight test work. The water, which can be pumped around the system, represents not only interior and passenger weight, but also differing center of gravity positions. The first aircraft in the test program to have a representative interior was MSN002, the third to join the effort. This was given the job of cabin system testing, including environmental control system, lighting, noise, water, and waste tests. Its first flight was a short hop to Hamburg for fitting out with a representative cabin seating up to 520. *Airbus*

The heads of the airlines and operators also spoke up. ILFC's Steve Udvar-Hazy hailed the A380 as the "beginning of a new era in civil aviation," and said that it represents "the direction the airline industry is going: mass transportation on a global scale." FedEx Chairman, President, and Chief Executive Fred Smith said, "2008 can't come quickly enough for us. The aircraft is pretty close to perfect. It gives us a lot more cubic space, a lot more payload, and a lot more range, but it also sits in almost the same parking dimension as our largest aircraft today and only utilizes one slot. That's a great advantage."

Sheikh Ahmed bin Saeed Al-Maktoum, chairman of Emirates, the largest single A380 customer, confirmed the aircraft was "a key element" in the future growth of the Dubai–based carrier because of the "continued constraints on traffic rights and the availability of landing slots." Despite the incredible size of the Emirates A380 fleet growth plan, which includes up to 45 aircraft (including two from ILFC), Sheikh Ahmed added that "every single one of the A380s we have ordered has been carefully prepared for and supports present and future network needs." Akbar Al Baker, chief executive of neighboring airline Qatar Airways, stressed the interior flexibility offered by an aircraft with more floor space than any airliner in history. "We are looking at having innovations that other airlines have not yet thought about yet."

Echoing these sentiments, Virgin Chairman Sir Richard Branson said the A380 would give operators the chance to provide a new level of service. "The A380 can take up to 900 passengers, but at Virgin we plan to only have about 500 passengers." Branson added the Virgin aircraft would feature beauty parlors and ". . . larger bars, so passengers are not stuck in their seats and can get out and meet each other." The aircraft would also have casinos for gambling as well as a few private double beds "so there will be at least two ways to get lucky!" he joked.

The reveal also generated massive interest around the world. As television networks such as CNN and Sky TV beamed live pictures to screens on every continent, an unprecedented 640,000 unique visitors logged on to the Airbus website. Interestingly, more than one in three visitors came from the United States despite the time difference, while the next largest proportion came from the United Kingdom; Germany, Sweden, Spain, Netherlands, and France followed. Overall, over 14 million hits were recorded by the site through the day.

Inevitably, some of the news on the world's websites was not good reading for Airbus. Although most credited the engineering achievement, some news reporters picked up on acknowledgments by EADS the previous month that the estimated cost overruns on the project were now about €1.45 billion (U.S. $1.92 billion). Forgeard had set the figure at the slightly more conservative €1.0 billion (U.S. $1.7 billion) over a longer time period up to 2010 that, given the overall €11 billion (U.S. $15.9 billion) estimate on the total development costs, was deemed acceptable.

According to Forgeard, this also meant the provisional break-even target was 250 sales, assuming a relatively benign flight test effort and smooth entry-into-service from the first quarter of 2006 onward. At the reveal, however, Forgeard told the Irish Radio station RTL, "We'll sell a lot more than 250. We'll sell 700 or 750. You know it is a plane that will fly for 30 or 40 years."

The following day, January 19, the whole show was repeated for the benefit of more than

The world's longest airliner meets the world's largest airliner. Pictured on arrival for the first time at *l'abreuvoir*, or "cattle trough," as the Airbus flight test center is called, the sheer bulk of the A380 became apparent when MSN001 was drawn up alongside the A340-600 prototype. At 245 feet, 11 inches in length, the A340-600 remains the longest airliner ever built—but only just. The single-decker is 3 feet longer than the 777-300 and 8 feet longer than the A380. In every other way, however, there was no beating the A380 for bragging rights! *Airbus*

Despite taking off at a staggering weight of 928,300 pounds, a world record for a civil airliner, the aircraft was eerily quiet. Nearby witnesses noticed the biggest airliner ever to leave the surface of the planet had just flown overhead making significantly less noise than the far smaller A320 twin-engined airliner that had left the runway just a short while before. Climbing straight ahead, Rosay etracted flaps, slats, and undercarriage at 10,000 feet before continuing to almost 14,000 feet on a track that took it south and west toward Tarbes and the Pyrenees for the second phase of the test flight. *Mark Wagner*

Backing up to the "Bikini" area for engine start-up, MSN001 underwent several weeks of ground tests in the run-up to first flight. These included slow- and high-speed accelerations and sudden stops, brake and thrust reverser tests, engine runs, and taxi tests. Taxi speed limits in service are expected to be 15 miles per hour. The initial pair of test aircraft was each fitted with more than 44,000 pounds of test gear, wired together with 210 miles of cabling. *Mark Wagner*

50,000 Airbus employees around the world, about 5,000 of which packed the hall for a re-run of the spectacular sound and light show. The crowd was mostly made up of employees who had won a place at the event through a prize draw, and included a driver for Airbus China in Beijing who was made his first journey away from his native country to attend the ceremony.

With the big show over, the gleaming blue-and-white behemoth, registered appropriately F-WWOW, was returned to the cold outside to continue the build-up to outfitting for flight tests. Known as station 18, this phase concerned fuel and pressurization tests and was followed by a visit to station 22 for a final systems and equipment upgrade. The program received a boost in late January when China

Southern officially ordered five A380s, the first couple of which would be delivered in time to help the airline take passengers to Beijing for the 2008 Olympics. The latest sale took overall firm orders to 154 aircraft from 15 customers.

Meanwhile, ground vibration tests of MSN002, which would be the third to fly, were completed after validating frequency and structural damping modes used in models for upcoming flutter clearance flights. Tests dragged on through February and March, and it was not until April 6 that the aircraft was finally handed over to flight test and the final pre-first-flight work at station 17.

Engines and APU were powered up, with the de-storage of oil from the engine oil system causing spectacular white exhaust clouds behind the aircraft on April 8. The following day, the aircraft trundled to Runway 32L at Toulouse for its first low-speed rolling taxi tests. These continued through the second and third weeks of April with higher and higher speed accelerations, and the use of thrust reversers noted on April 13. Although hopes were raised for a first flight on April 18 and again on April 20, the weather refused to cooperate and it was not until the last week of April that things looked better.

Finally, on the morning of April 27, the omens looked perfect for the long-awaited maiden flight attempt. A ridge of high pressure moved into France from the Atlantic bringing clear skies, warm weather, and a gentle northerly breeze that would allow the A380 to take off away from the city of Toulouse, a vital requirement before the attempt could be sanctioned.

Flight Division Senior Vice President Captain Claude Lelaie and Chief Test Pilot Captain Jacques Rosay led the six-man crew; between them, Lelaie and Rosay had already amassed more than 13,000 flight test hours, including the first flights of the A318, A340-500, and -600. Flight Test Division Vice President Fernando Alonso was picked as flight test engineer responsible for overseeing flight controls and aircraft structural monitoring, while the others included flight test engineers Jacky Joye, Manfred Birnfeld, and Gerard Desbois.

The word spread around the world that first flight was imminent, and by the early hours of the morning crowds estimated by the police to number about 50,000 packed the fields and roads around

Flaps down and slats out, MSN001 appeared almost to glide silently overhead as it completed a surprise fly past to the delight of the 50,000 people gathered on and around Toulouse's Blagnac Airport on April 27, 2005. The three huge sections of single-slotted Fowler flaps have a combined surface area of more than 70.5 square feet per wing and can be set by a combined slat/flap lever with six detent positions. The first setting, position "0," is for climb, cruise, or holding and is zero deflection on all slats and flaps. Position "1" is for holding and puts slats at 20 degrees and the droop nose at 22. Position "1+F" is for takeoff and sets the slats at 20, droop nose at 22, and flaps at 8 degrees. Position "2" for more demanding takeoffs and sets the slats at 20, droop nose at 22, and flaps at 17 degrees, while position "3"—shown in this photo—puts all three at 23, 25, and 22 degrees, respectively. Maximum flap angle, at position "Full" is 33 degrees of flap for landing, with slats at 23 and the droop nose at 25 degrees. *Mark Wagner*

With the bulk of the early flight test program responsibilities on its shoulders, MSN001 was expected to conduct about 600 hours of the planned 2,100-hour test effort for the Trent 900-powered A380. This program would also involve three other aircraft: MSN002, 004, and 007. The second aircraft to fly, MSN004 was scheduled to focus on performance tests and particularly takeoff and landing evaluations, including water ingestion tests on a flooded section of runway at Istres, the French air force flight test center near Marseille in the south of France. It was also tasked with "hot and high" performance work, normally involving a trip to "El Alto" the 13,450-foot-high airport at La Paz, the capitol of Bolivia, and cold soak tests in either Siberia or Canada—depending on where the coldest weather could be found. *Mark Wagner*

Touchdown! The world's first superjumbo landing took place at 14:23 local time, completing a very successful 3-hour and 54-minute maiden flight. The A380 had loomed out of the clear sky to the south and completed a fly past before making a climbing right turn and joining a wide, right-hand circuit, the faithful Corvette in attendance the whole time. The landing was made on runway 32L, the longer of the two parallel strips at Toulouse. No thrust reverser was used to help stop the aircraft, which braked to a halt using maximum flap, slat, and brake settings. *Mark Wagner*

Toulouse's Blagnac Airport. Under a cloudless sky, the crew boarded the giant blue-and-white aircraft and started F-WWOW's four Trent 900 engines. Shortly after 10:00 a.m. local time, the aircraft taxied slowly to the holding point of 32L and then onto the runway itself.

Easing forward the throttles until they reached maximum power, Lelaie and Rosay guided the A380 down the centerline as it quickly gathered speed. At 10:29 a.m., Rosay pulled back on the side stick controller and the aircraft launched effortlessly into the air. At liftoff, the ballasted aircraft weighed 927,000 pounds—instantly winning the A380 a place in the record books with the heaviest ever takeoff of a commercial airliner!

Accompanied by the Airbus flight test chase plane, an Aerospatiale Corvette, the aircraft flew straight ahead until, to the awestruck on-lookers at Toulouse, it simply dwindled into a dot. At about 10,000 feet Rosay retracted the landing gear, slats, and flaps before climbing farther to almost 14,000 feet for initial handling qualities tests. The first part of the flight, including the takeoff, had been conducted in direct law, in which the flight control system's (FCS) envelope protection features are disabled. Later on in the flight, the FCS normal law was activated for a while.

The crew reported from the air that the aircraft was handling well, while flight test engineer Fernando Alonso reported that "in every configuration there was very little buffet." With several initial handling and flight control law tests completed, the crew headed back to Toulouse where MSN001 landed smoothly to rapturous applause and cheers some 3 hours and 54 minutes after taking off.

After all the back-patting and congratulating were over, the crew admitted this was where the hard work really began. Ahead of them lay a 2,500-hour test effort that was expected to last about 13 months. MSN001 was the first of four aircraft scheduled to take part in the flight test and certification effort for the Rolls-Royce Trent 900-powered version scheduled to culminate with the delivery of the first aircraft to SIA toward the end of 2006. Beyond that, lay the follow-on certification program for the Engine Alliance GP7200-powered version later in 2006, and the freighter variant beyond that.

The tests would stretch the A380 to the very limits. MSN001 and 004 would perform the bulk of the tests with 600 flight test hours due to be chalked up by each of them by mid-2006. The second pair, MSN002 and 007, would between them be scheduled to contribute about 900 hours of testing to the program, including critical work on the cabin systems and early long flights with full passenger loads of staff volunteers, and later route proving.

Tests ranged from takeoff and climb performance and stalls, to wake vortex effects, braking and rejected takeoff performance, cross wind landings, noise certification, cold and hot weather tests, emergency evacuation work, and "hot and high" performance evaluation.

However, the first flight took place at least a month later than Airbus originally planned, and inevitably Airbus faced the fact that deliveries would not be able to take place as scheduled. First details of the slippage emerged in May 2005 when the company revealed that it was sending out teams to "negotiate" revised delivery times with the initial aircraft customers. Singapore Airlines—the first to take the aircraft for commercial services—still hoped to have its initial deliveries by the end of 2006 but knew that the chances of making it by December that year would be tight.

Others immediately affected by the slippage included Emirates and Qantas, the latter being advised that first deliveries would begin in April 2007 rather than October the previous year. It was not only the delays to the start of flight tests that had complicated the schedule but also the intense work of finalizing cabin configurations. Air France also acknowledged it was talking to Airbus and revising its acceptance schedule, having originally planned to take first delivery in April 2007.

The team knew it faced a truly mammoth task for a mammoth aircraft. However, given its success to-date and the gritty determination it had showed to overcome the odds and develop the A380 in the first place, Airbus was convinced it was up to the task. It accepted that the schedule had been tight to begin with but vowed to catch up as quickly as it could and ensure that the entry into service would be as smooth as possible. They knew the A380 was a world beater . . . now they were out to prove it.

Proud moments as the flight test crew, accompanied down the extremely long stairway from the aircraft by Airbus Chief Executive Noel Forgeard and A380 Program Executive Vice President Charles Champion (nearer the top), acknowledges the applause from the crowd after first flight. Leading the crew was Airbus Chief Test Pilot Jacques Rosay (waving) and Flight Division Senior Vice President Claude Lelaie. The remaining four flight test engineers were Airbus Flight Test Division Vice President Fernando Alonso, and engineers Gerard Desbois, Manfred Birnfeld, and Jacky Joye. *Mark Wagner*

The world's first superjumbo rests after its first flight. With the pressure on getting deliveries going by late 2006, the test team had its work cut out. Even after completing certification of the Trent 900-powered A380-800, a feat that was expected around mid-2006, Airbus still faced the challenge of repeating certification of the Engine Alliance GP7200-powered version starting later that year. Right on the heels of these milestones comes the development, test, and certification of the -800F freighter and beyond that possibly the stretch -900. Whatever the exact sequence, Airbus and its partners hope the A380 program will be keeping them busy for years and years to come. *Mark Wagner*

Captain Jacques Rosay described the superjumbo as being as easy to handle as a bicycle. "This aircraft is very, very easy to fly. Any Airbus pilot will feel immediately at ease with this aircraft, a pure member of the Airbus family." He was enthusiastic about the flight deck design, which he described as "an excellent cockpit" that makes ". . . the work for the crew easier and safer. "He added that, following the successful start of the flight test program, "the Airbus shareholders can sleep easy now." *Mark Wagner*

APPENDIX
A380 Specifications

SPECIFICATIONS	A380-800	A380-800F
Fuselage Diameter	23 feet, 5 inches/7.1 meters	23 feet, 5 inches/7.1 meters
Overall Length	239 feet, 3 inches/72.9 meters	239 feet, 3 inches/72.9 meters
Wingspan	261 feet, 8 inches/79.8 meters	261 feet, 8 inches/79.8 meters
Overall Height	79 feet, 7 inches/24.3 meters	79 feet, 7 inches/24.3 meters
Wing Area	9,104 square feet/845.8 square meters	9,104 square feet/845.8 square meters
Wing Sweep	33.5 degrees	33.5 degrees
Cruise Speed (Mach)	0.85	0.85
Maximum Operating Speed (Mach)	0.89	0.89
CAPACITY		
Passenger (typical 3-class layout)	555 (22 first, 96 business, 437 economy)	None
Maximum Passenger Capacity	853	N/A
Cargo Containers (LD3)	38	17 pallets on upper deck, 29 M1 pallets on main deck, 38 LD3 or 13 pallets on lower deck
Cargo Load	33,000 pounds/14,968.5 kilograms	335,000 pounds/151,953.4 kilograms
Range	8,000 U.S. nautical miles/7,994.9 UK nautical miles	5,600 nautical miles/5,596.4 nautical miles
WEIGHT AND FUEL		
Maximum Take-off Weight	1,235,000 pounds/560,185.6 kilograms	1,300,000 pounds/589,670.1 kilograms
Maximum Landing Weight	851,000 pounds/386,007.1 kilograms	941,000 pounds/426,830.4 kilograms
Maximum Payload (Structural)	185,000 pounds/83,914.6 kilograms	331,000 pounds/150,139.1 kilograms
Maximum Fuel Capacity	81,890 U.S. gallons/309,987.4 liters	81,890 U.S. gallons/309,987.4 liters
MILESTONES		
Launch	December 2000	December 2000
First Flight	April 27, 2005	Mid-2007
Entry into Service	Late 2006	Late 2008
POWERPLANTS		
Engine Alliance		
GP7270 (A380-800)	70,000 pounds (311kN) thrust	
GP7277 (A380-800F)	76,800 pounds (340kN) thrust	
GP7682 (A380 growth)	81,500 pounds (362kN) thrust	
Rolls-Royce		
Trent 970 (A380-800)	70,000 pounds (311kN) thrust	
Trent 977 (A680-800F)	77,000 pounds (342kN) thrust	
Trent 980 (A380 growth)	84,000 pounds (374kN) thrust	

A380 Order Book (as of June 2005)

Customer	A380-800F	A380-800F	Option	Engine
Air France	10		4	GP7200
China Southern	5			TBA
Emirates	41	2		GP7200
Ethiad Airways	4			Trent 900
FedEx		10	10	GP7200
ILFC	5	5		GP7200
Kingfisher Airlines	5			TBA
Korean Air	5		3	GP7200
Lufthansa	15		10	Trent 900
Malaysia Airlines	6			Trent 900
Qantas	12		10	Trent 900
Qatar Airways	2		2	Trent 900
Signapore Airlines	10		15	Trent 900
Thai Airways Intl	6			TBA
UPS		10	10	TBA
Virgin Atlantic	6		6	Trent 900
Total	132	27	60	
Totals		159	60	

INDEX

A380-800 Main Structural (Parts) Components

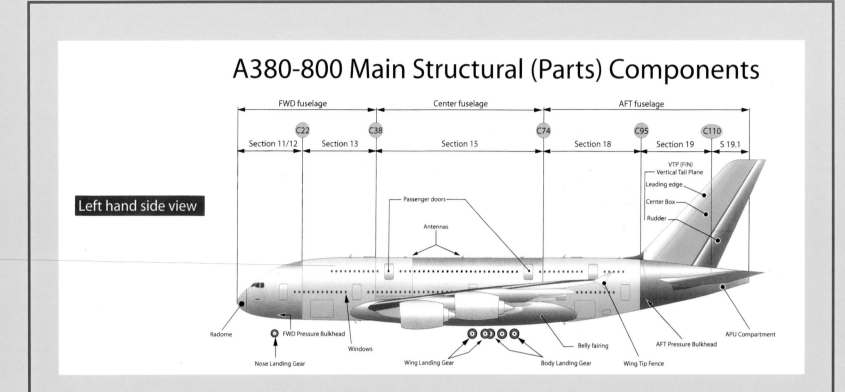

Left hand side view

FWD fuselage | Center fuselage | AFT fuselage

Section 11/12 | Section 13 | Section 15 | Section 18 | Section 19 | S 19.1

C22 · C38 · C74 · C95 · C110

VTP (FIN) — Vertical Tail Plane
Leading edge
Center Box
Rudder

Passenger doors
Antennas

Radome
FWD Pressure Bulkhead
Nose Landing Gear
Windows
Wing Landing Gear
Body Landing Gear
Belly fairing
Wing Tip Fence
AFT Pressure Bulkhead
APU Compartment

A380-800 fuselage cross section comparisons

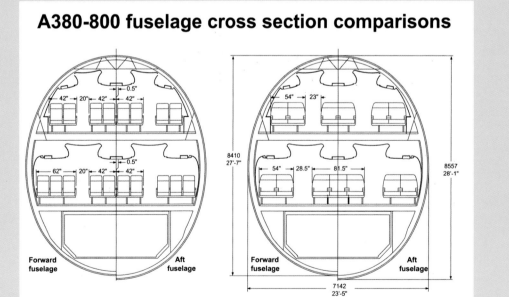

Economy class

42" 20" 42" 42" — 0.5"
62" 20" 42" 42" — 0.5"

Forward fuselage — Aft fuselage

April 2003

Business class

54" 23"
54" 28.5" 81.5"

8410 27'-7"
8557 28'-1"
7142 23'-5"

Forward fuselage — Aft fuselage